tapas

Louise Pickford

photography by Sandra Lane

hamlyn

Publishing Director: Alison Goff

Senior Editor: Sasha Judelson
Assistant Editor: Katey Day
Commissioning Editor: Nicola Hill

Art Director: Keith Martin
Senior Designer: Louise Leffler

Photographer: Sandra Lane
Home Economist: Louise Pickford
Stylist: Mary Nordan
Indexer: Hilary Bird

Production Controller: Karina Han

Notes
All recipes serve 4 unless otherwise stated

Standard level spoon measurements are used in all recipes.
1 tablespoon = one 15 ml spoon
1 teaspoon = one 5 ml spoon

Both imperial and metric measurements have been given in all recipes.
Use one set of measurements only and not a mixture of both.

Eggs should be medium unless otherwise stated.

Milk should be full fat unless otherwise stated.

Fresh herbs should be used unless otherwise stated. If unavailable use
dried herbs as an alternative but halve the quantities stated.

Ovens should be preheated to the specified temperature – if using a fan
assisted oven, follow the manufacturer's instructions for adjusting the
time and temperature.

Tapas
Louise Pickford

First published in 1997 by
Hamlyn
a division of Octopus Publishing Group Limited
2–4 Heron Quays, London E14 4JP

Reprinted 1999

This paperback edition published in 2001

Copyright © 1997, 2001

British Library Cataloguing-in-Publication Data
A catalogue record for this book is available from the British Library

ISBN 0 600 60541 8

Main text set in 10 on 14pt Linotype Sabon

Produced by Toppan, Hong Kong
Printed in China

contents

introduction

At the heart of Spanish traditions is a ritual carried out daily with typical Mediterranean passion: the eating of tapas – a small snack washed down with a glass of chilled sherry or wine – takes places in bars all over Spain at both lunchtime and then again in the early evening.

The word 'tapa' from which tapas derives, translates literally as 'cover' and as the story goes, bar owners would serve their customers a drink with a slice of bread covering the top of the glass. This rather bizarre custom was most probably done for a very good reason, to prevent insects from enjoying the drink between sips! The bread was then eaten and was soon topped with a slice of ham or cheese, and here the whole custom of tapas was born.

To most of us (except the Spanish of course) tapas probably evokes memories of holidays abroad. After a day relaxing in the sun, a thirst quenching drink and a little nibble seem a perfect way to enjoy those last few hours of sunlight. Small tables spill out of the bars onto pavements and many a tourist and local alike sit and chatter cheerfully with a chilled drink in one hand and a plate of roasted nuts or chilli-spiked olives in the other. Whenever I travel abroad I am instantly drawn to the street foods and snacks that are far more common place than at home. Many of these dishes are finger foods, making them practical to eat whilst meandering through the narrow streets. I find it much more interesting to nibble on a number of small morsels, with a range of exciting flavours and textures.

Tapas can also be enjoyed when entertaining at home. Whether you are hosting a drinks party, a formal dinner or a casual gathering of close friends, handing around a tray of finger foods will always be appreciated. As well as receiving praise from your guests, there are practical benefits in preparing tapas yourself. A few nibbles with drinks can often mean serving two rather than three courses at dinner; so the extra time spent on the nibbles may well save you time later on!

Tapas is divided into six practical chapters and offers a much broader collection of dishes than just Spanish-style tapas. Appetizers, nibbles and snacks from all over the world have been brought together to produce a comprehensive recipe book with tapas for every occasion.

Each chapter is self-explanatory which offers the reader instant access to the type of recipe required. **One Bite**, the first chapter contains literally dishes of small nibbles which can be eaten in one go. Recipes include Salted Almonds, Spicy Glazed Cashews and Root Vegetable Crisps. These really are the perfect partner to a glass of chilled wine or sherry and should be arranged in small dishes or on napkins, to sit neatly on a tray or platter as the drinks are handed around. Toothpicks are useful to spike oily foods such as Marinated Olives, but make sure you have a saucer or empty dish to hand for the olive stones!

Two Bites provides a wide range of really exciting recipes with just that bit more to

them. Melting Polenta Triangle Sandwiches and Cheese Stuffed Filo Fingers are ideal if you are hosting a drinks party when it is often a good idea to offer slightly more substantial dishes to eat. Tasty food and good wine are after all convivial to happy banter and a successful party! Interesting, new recipe ideas can be found here, including Chilli Fried Panisse and the Smoked Mussel Fritters.

The third chapter, **Bigger Bites**, offers dishes that are ideal as a light lunch or supper dish which can also be served as a starter. Alternatively, lay out a selection of five or six dishes 'mezze-style' so everyone can help themselves. There are some old favourites to be found like the Piedmontese Peppers and Spanish Tortilla, intermingled with a few more unusual recipes such as the Anchovy Stuffed Courgette Flowers and Rolled Skewered Sole Fillets with Tomatoes and Mozzarella.

Little Dishes personifies Spain and the tapas tradition more than any other chapter, with its collection of dishes served in small bowls, plates and saucers (or in some cases shells) in a typical Spanish manner. Unlike most of the other chapters, however, you will need a fork or chopsticks to eat the food. These recipes are versatile and lend themselves perfectly to a casual dinner when you could perhaps serve six different dishes. As the whole feeling is more Spanish you will find several classic tapas dishes including Potato Bravas, Kidneys cooked with Sherry and Broad Beans with Serrano Ham. If you are feeling more adventurous try the Pacific Rim Mussels or the Marinated Herring with Horseradish Cream.

Most of the dishes in **Breads and Pastries** are substantial enough to be served as a light meal, starter or snack. There are several kinds of crostini or bruschetta recipes including the more unusual dish, Prawn and Rocket Piadina. A piadina is an Italian wheat tortilla which was in fact the precursor to the pizza base, and it provides a delicious base for the prawn topping. Several of the dishes make ideal picnic foods, particularly the Pan Bagnat Slices and the Picnic Chicken Loaf – just before you set off wrap them in waxed paper, they always look fabulous in the bright sunshine.

The final chapter, **Sauces, Oils and Dips**, as the title suggests, includes those recipes found in other parts of the book as well as recipes in their own right. The oils can all be served with fresh bread to dip, which I think always makes a lovely starter or appetizer and helps your guests relax around the dinner table. The Bagna Cauda (a classic Italian anchovy sauce) is traditionally served hot, in its own dish at the table, but without that traditional serving dish I simply transfer it to a separate dish and serve it warm with a selection of baby vegetables.

Despite this book's obvious links with a long serving and wonderful tradition I have tried to give it a far more modern feel, emphasized by a collection of international recipes and by the light and colourful photography as well as a simple, modern design. All of these factors come together to make a book which I hope will inspire cooks and satisfy the eaters!

Opposite from top left clockwise: Mini Chicken Kiev (see page 56); Roasted Vine Tomatoes with Goats Cheese (see page 90); Chickpea and Chard Tortilla (see page 60); and Grilled Sweetcorn with Flavoured Butters (see page 40)

glossary of ingredients

Bulghar wheat
This grain is partially processed by boiling until cracked and is often referred to as cracked wheat. This process enables the grain to absorb liquid more readily and reduces the cooking time. It is used extensively in North African, Greek, Turkish and Middle Eastern cookery.

Chard
A member of the beet family, this green leaf vegetable has a thick white central stalk, which should be discarded before cooking. It can be served as a vegetable on its own and is particularly nice steamed and tossed with extra virgin olive oil, salt, pepper and lemon juice.

Chickpea flour
Also called besan or gram flour this is the finely milled, pale yellow flour made from roasted chickpeas. It is used extensively in Indian cooking but can be found in French, North African and Middle Eastern dishes.

Chorizo
This is the Spanish pork sausage made with paprika which gives it a distinctive red colour. Chorizo can be mild or highly spiced, it is usually cured and can be eaten raw.

Coconut cream
More authentic than canned coconut milk, UHT coconut cream is available in small cartons from some supermarkets or oriental food stores. Use creamed coconut dissolved in boiling water as a substitute.

Courgette flowers
The flowers of the courgette plant (part of the marrow family) are rarely seen in Britain unless you are fortunate enough to grow your own. Courgette flowers are far more common in the Mediterranean countries where they are stuffed and baked as well as deep-fried.

Dried broad beans
Also called fava, these dried beans are available from most Middle Eastern, Greek or Turkish food stores. Dried butter beans can be substituted, if necessary.

Dried shiitake mushrooms
As the name suggests these are fresh shiitake mushrooms that have been dried. These are available in some supermarkets and the larger variety can be found in oriental food shops.

Fontina
An Italian cows' milk cheese which comes from the high alpine meadows of the Valle d'Aosta. It is a pale creamy cheese with a deep rust-brown rind, and a delicate nutty flavour. Fontina melts well when heated and mozzarella can be used as an alternative. Fontina is available from Italian food stores or good cheese suppliers.

Kefalotyri
This is a strongly flavoured Greek ewes' milk cheese (although occasionally made from goats' milk). It has a sharp, slightly acidic flavour and is mostly used grated in cooked dishes. Pecorino Sardo makes a good alternative.

Lime leaves
Aromatic lime leaves from the Kaffir lime are widely used in Thai and Indonesian cooking. Lime leaves are available from some supermarkets and oriental food stores. Pared lime rind can be substituted.

Pancetta
An Italian streaky bacon which comes both smoked and unsmoked. Other streaky bacon can be used as an alternative.

Pasta flour
A highly graded extra fine wheat flour used to make pasta dough. Available from Italian food stores and some supermarkets.

Pecorino Sardo
Pecorino, an Italian hard cheese, is the Italian generic term for ewes' milk cheese. Pecorino Sardo is made in Sardinia, it is similar to Parmesan in both flavour and texture.

Pimento
This is the name for the sweet red Spanish peppers available dried or in cans.

Plantain

This is a vegetable but actually belongs to the banana family. It is indigenous to the Caribbean, Central and South America and is much more bland and starchier than the banana. Plantains need cooking in order to bring out their flavour. Buy ripe plantains which will have turned from green through to yellow and then black whilst ripening.

Prosecco

This is an Italian sparkling wine which is very light and delicate. A Cava or methode champenoise may be substituted.

Reblochon

A semi-soft French mountain cheese with a deep yellow rind, it is shaped in small rounds and set on wooden discs. Reblochon has a wonderful deep fruity flavour and cooks well. Camembert or Brie can be used instead.

Rice vinegar

Made from fermented rice wine, this vinegar is used extensively in Far Eastern cookery. Sherry vinegar can be used as an alternative.

Salt cod

This is cod that has been gutted and cleaned and then soaked in brine, preserved in salt and dried. It is principally from the Scandinavian countries although it is prepared throughout the Mediterranean. It needs to be soaked for at least 24 hours before cooking.

Serrano ham

This is similar to *Prosciutto di Parma* but is from Serrano in Spain.

Smoked mozzarella

As the name suggests this is simply mozzarella that has been smoked. It is not readily available although good cheese suppliers and some Italian delicatessens will stock it.

Tahini

This is the paste made from grinding roasted sesame seeds and is sold in jars. It will separate with age so stir well before use. Tahini is available from Middle Eastern stores and most large supermarkets.

Thai fish sauce

This is the salt of Thai cooking and is also known as nam pla. It is made from fermented fish and is used extensively in Thai dishes. Use light soy sauce as an alternative.

Vermicelli rice noodles

Made from rice, these noodles are a staple diet in southern China, they are used in soups as well as meat, fish and vegetable dishes. Follow the packet instructions for soaking.

SEAFOOD PREPARATION

Some of the recipes in the book require pre-pared fresh seafood; it is best to follow these simple instructions if preparing them yourself.

Cooked crab

Twist off the claws and legs of the crab, crack open and pick out the meat and reserve. Holding the shell in your hands press down firmly against the tail section until it breaks away. Pull out and discard the stomach and gills found just behind the mouth and the feathery beards, either side of the body. Scrape out the dark shell meat and pick out the white meat from the body cavity.

Fresh mussels

Scrub well to remove any mud and tiny shells attached to the mussels. Wash well and pull out the scraggly beards that often remain hanging from the closed shell. Tap the mussels gently and discard any that remain open as these are dead.

Fresh oysters

Ask your fishmonger to shuck (open) the oysters for you. Carefully snip the muscle that attaches them to their shell.

Raw prawns

To remove the intestine, cut off the head and peel away the shells and legs. With a sharp knife cut along the back of each prawn and pull out the black vein which is the intestine. Wash and dry well.

Fresh scallops

If the scallops are still in their shells ask your fishmonger to clean them for you. Take the shelled scallop and cut away the protruding tough muscle from each one and remove the dark vein. Wash and dry well.

Squid

Hold the squid body gently and then pull away from you; most of the squid body innards should come out and should then be discarded. Cut off the tentacles, removing the sharp beak and reserve. The skin should now peel away easily, pull out the transparent quill like cartilage from the back of each squid. Wash out the body and then cut into thin rings, dry well by patting gently all over with kitchen paper.

Clockwise from far left: Caraway Crackers; Garlic, Chive Sables; and Spicy Palmiers

Serve your guests a selection of the following morsels as you pass around pre-dinner drinks. Spike the Marinated Olives, Chorizo Sausage with Bread and the Pork, Parma Ham and Sage Rolls with cocktail sticks for ease.

one bite

Makes: 24 Palmiers
Preparation time: 10 minutes
Cooking time: 15 minutes

spicy palmiers

Both variations of this recipe make a tasty pre-dinner snack.

250 g/8 oz puff pastry,
   defrosted if frozen
2 tablespoons olive oil
½ teaspoon paprika
pinch ground cayenne
3 tablespoons freshly grated
   Parmesan cheese

- Roll out the puff pastry thinly on a lightly floured surface and trim to make a 20 x 25 cm/8 x 10 inch rectangle.
- Combine the oil, paprika, cayenne and Parmesan and brush three-quarters of the paste all over the pastry to give an even coating.
- Fold both long sides of pastry in to meet in the middle, spread over a layer of the remaining paste and fold the pastry in half lengthways. Press down firmly.
- Using a sharp knife cut into 24 thin slices and transfer, cut side down, to 2 greased baking sheets.
- Bake in a preheated oven, 200°C (400°F), Gas Mark 6, for 10 minutes, turn over and bake for a further 4–5 minutes until the pastries are crisp and golden. Cool on a wire rack. These are best eaten the same day.

variation
anchovy palmiers

250 g/8 oz puff pastry,
   defrosted if frozen
2 tablespoons Anchoïade (see
   page 124)

- Follow the method above but replace the filling with the Anchoïade.

Preparation time: 10 minutes
Cooking time: 15 minutes

Makes: 28–30
Preparation time: 5 minutes, plus chilling time
Cooking time: 15 minutes

garlic, chive *sables*

- Sift the flour and salt into a bowl and rub in the butter until the mixture resembles fine breadcrumbs.
- Work in the cream cheese, garlic, chives and 1–2 tablespoons of cold water to form a soft dough. Knead lightly, wrap in cling film and chill for 30 minutes.
- Roll the pastry out thinly on a lightly floured surface and using a 6.5 cm/2½ inch pastry cutter, stamp out rounds. Re-roll the pastry trimmings and repeat to make 28–30 rounds. Transfer to 2 baking sheets.
- Brush lightly with the beaten egg and bake in a preheated oven, 200°C (400°F), Gas Mark 6, for 15 minutes until golden. Cool on a wire rack. These are best when eaten the same day.

175 g/6 oz plain flour
a pinch of salt
75 g/3 oz butter, diced
25 g/1 oz cream cheese
1 garlic clove, crushed
2 tablespoon chopped fresh chives
1 small egg, beaten

caraway crackers

Serve these savoury crackers as a nibble with an aperitif, or with cheese. Fennel seeds can be substituted for the caraway seeds, if liked.

- Sift the plain flour, salt and cumin into a bowl. Rub in the butter until the mixture resembles fine breadcrumbs.
- Stir in the caraway seeds and then gradually work in 2–3 tablespoons water to form a soft dough.
- Knead lightly until smooth, cover with cling film and leave to rest for 30 minutes.
- Roll the dough out thinly on a lightly floured surface and using a 7 cm/3 inch pastry cutter, stamp out rounds. Re-roll once and repeat to make 16–18 rounds.
- Transfer the crackers to a large baking sheet, prick the surfaces with a fork and bake in a preheated oven, 190°C (375°F), Gas Mark 5, for 10 minutes. Turn the crackers over and bake for a further 5 minutes until crisp and lightly golden. Cool on a wire rack and store in an airtight container for up to 2 days.

125 g/4 oz plain flour
¼ teaspoon salt
½ teaspoon ground cumin
50 g/2 oz butter, diced
1–2 teaspoons caraway seeds, according to taste

Makes: 16–18
Preparation time: 15–20 minutes, plus resting time
Cooking time: 15 minutes

250 g/8 oz large whole green
   olives
2 garlic cloves, sliced
grated rind ½ lemon
1 tablespoon balsamic vinegar
½ teaspoon chilli flakes
4 tablespoons extra virgin
   olive oil

marinated olives

○ Place the olives in a bowl, add the remaining ingredients and stir well. Cover and refrigerate for up to 3 days.

Serves: 8
Preparation time: 5 minutes

250 g/8 oz mixed whole
   green and black olives
1 garlic clove, crushed
1 teaspoon grated ginger
2 lime leaves, shredded or
   grated rind 1 lime
2 red chillies, bruised
2 tablespoons dark soy sauce
extra virgin olive oil, to cover

variation
olives marinated with Asian flavours

○ Place all the ingredients in a bowl and stir well. Cover and refrigerate for up to 1 week.

Serves: 8
Preparation time: 5 minutes

salted almonds

- Heat the oil in a small, heavy-based frying pan, add the nuts in several batches and stir-fry over a medium heat until evenly browned.
- Using a slotted spoon transfer the nuts to a bowl and add plenty of sea salt. Stir to coat the nuts and store in an airtight container for up to 3 days.

6 tablespoons olive oil
250 g/8 oz blanched almonds
sea salt

Serves: 4
Preparation time: 2 minutes
Cooking time: 5 minutes

variation
spicy glazed cashews

- Melt the butter in a small, heavy-based frying pan and then stir in the honey, salt and cayenne along with 1 tablespoon of water. Bring to the boil.
- Add the cashew nuts and stir over a medium heat for 5 minutes until the nuts are toasted and well coated with the glaze. Tip out onto a greased baking sheet and leave to cool. These are best eaten the same day.

25 g/1 oz unsalted butter
3 tablespoons clear honey
1 teaspoon salt
¼ teaspoon cayenne pepper
250 g/8 oz cashew nuts

Serves: 8
Preparation time: 3 minutes
Cooking time: 6–7 minutes

Makes: approximately 12 falafel
Preparation time: 10 minutes, plus overnight soaking and chilling time
Cooking time: 6–8 minutes

125 g/4 oz dried broad beans, soaked overnight in cold water
2 tablespoons Greek yogurt
1 tablespoon tahini paste
1 tablespoon lemon juice
1 garlic clove, crushed
1 teaspoon ground coriander
½ teaspoon ground cumin
½ teaspoon cayenne pepper
1 tablespoon chopped fresh coriander
1 tablespoon chopped fresh mint
salt and pepper
vegetable oil, for shallow-frying
Greek yogurt, to serve

falafel

These savoury patties are a traditional Middle Eastern snack. The mixture is quite wet and crumbly when you come to shape them, but this ensures a perfect, light texture once fried.

- Drain the broad beans and dry thoroughly. Place in a food processor and blend to form a fairly smooth paste, transfer the puréed beans to a bowl. Stir in all the remaining ingredients and season with salt and pepper, cover and chill for 1 hour.
- Form the mixture into small patties. Heat a shallow layer of oil in a non-stick frying pan and fry the patties a few at a time for 1–2 minutes on each side until golden. Serve with Greek yogurt.

root
vegetable crisps

These trendy nineties crisps are easy to make at home, and of course this means you can use your own favourite root vegetables.

- Slice the vegetables into fine wafers using a potato peeler or mandoline, keeping them in separate batches. (It is best to cut the carrots and parsnips lengthways.)
- Heat 5 cm/2 inches vegetable oil in a deep saucepan until it reaches 180–190°C (350–375°F), or until a cube of bread browns in 30 seconds. Pat the vegetables dry using kitchen paper.
- Again, keeping the vegetables separate, deep-fry them in batches for 30 seconds to 1½ minutes, until crisp and golden. Drain on kitchen paper and leave to cool on a wire rack.
- Transfer the crisps to a large bowl and sprinkle with sea salt and a little cayenne, if using. Pass the crisps around in small bowls.

2 beetroot
1 large potato
1 small sweet potato
2 carrots
2 parsnips
vegetable oil, for deep-frying
sea salt
cayenne pepper (optional)

Serves: 2–4
Preparation time: 10 minutes
Cooking time: 8–10 minutes

1 teaspoon fennel seeds
1 teaspoon pink peppercorns
250 g/8 oz goats' cheese, such
  as Sainte Maure
2 garlic cloves, peeled but left
  whole
2 small green chillies, bruised
2 sprigs fresh rosemary,
  bruised
2 bay leaves, bruised
extra virgin olive oil, to cover
crusty French bread, to serve

Serves: 8
Preparation time: 15 minutes

marinated
goats' cheese

The herbs and spices added to the oil infuse the goats' cheese as it marinates, giving it a wonderful delicate flavour.

- Put the fennel seeds and peppercorns in a small, heavy-based frying pan and heat gently until they start to pop and release an aroma. Leave to cool completely.
- Roll the cheese into small balls and place in a bowl or jar. Add the cooled fennel seeds and peppercorns, then add the remaining ingredients with sufficient olive oil to cover.
- Store in a cool place for at least 3 days, but no longer than 1 week. Serve the cheese balls with a little of the oil and chunks of French bread or spread on to slices of toasted French bread.

deep-fried
artichokes

You do not have to use baby artichokes for this dish. If you want to use larger artichokes pre-cook them before deep-frying them. Baby artichokes are available from good greengrocers or Mediterranean food shops.

12 baby artichokes

1 lemon, halved

vegetable oil, for deep-frying

4 tablespoons flour, seasoned
  with salt and pepper

salt, to serve

lemon wedges, to garnish

- Trim the artichokes and cut each one lengthways in half or quarters depending on the size. Rub all over the cut surface with the halved lemon.
- Heat 5 cm/2 inches vegetable oil in a deep frying pan until it reaches 180–190°C (350–375°F), or until a cube of bread browns in 30 seconds.
- Dip the artichokes in the seasoned flour to coat well and deep-fry in batches for 1–2 minutes until crisp and golden. Drain on kitchen paper. Serve sprinkled with salt and garnished with lemon wedges.

Serves: 4
Preparation time: 20 minutes
Cooking time: 1–2 minutes each batch

deep-fried
onion rings
in beer batter

These are far superior to any pre-prepared onion rings you can buy frozen, and are definitely worth making yourself at home.

- Slice the onions into 5 mm/¼ inch thick rings and separate out. Reserve all the larger rings and put the rest aside for use in another dish.
- In a bowl beat together the egg yolk, oil, beer and flour and season to taste with salt and pepper. Whisk the egg white until stiff and fold into the batter until evenly incorporated.
- Heat 5 cm/2 inches vegetable oil in a deep saucepan until it reaches 180–190°C (350–375°F), or until a cube of bread browns in 30 seconds. Dip the onion rings, a few at a time into the batter and then into the oil and deep-fry for 1–2 minutes until golden. Remove with a slotted spoon and drain on kitchen paper.
- Serve the onion rings hot with a bowl of Mayonnaise or Aïoli, to dip.

4 large onions
vegetable oil, for deep-frying
Mayonnaise or Aïoli, to serve
  (see page 125)

Batter:

1 egg, separated
1 tablespoon olive oil
100 ml/3½ fl oz light beer
65 g/2½ oz plain flour
salt and pepper

Serves: 4–6
Preparation time: 10 minutes
Cooking time: 10 minutes

deep-fried **mozzarella balls**

If you cannot find any mozzarella balls, which are known as boconcinni, buy a whole mozzarella and cut it into bite-sized chunks.

- Dry the mozzarella balls thoroughly using kitchen paper, then dip first in the seasoned flour, then the egg and finally the breadcrumbs. Chill for 30 minutes.
- Heat 5 cm/2 inches vegetable oil in a deep saucepan until it reaches 180–190°C (350–375°F), or until a cube of bread browns in 30 seconds. Deep-fry the mozzarella balls, in batches for 30 seconds to 1 minute until crisp and golden.
- Remove with a slotted spoon and drain on kitchen paper. Keep warm in the oven while cooking the remainer. Serve at once with the Smoky Tomato Salsa.

12 boconcinni mozzarella balls
2 tablespoons flour, seasoned with salt and pepper
1 egg, beaten
4 tablespoons dried bread-crumbs
vegetable oil, for deep-frying
1 quantity Smoky Tomato Salsa, to serve (see page 118)

Serves: 4
Preparation time: 5 minutes, plus chilling time
Cooking time: 30 seconds to 1 minute each

lamb and courgette koftas

Delicious served with a sweet relish or even redcurrant jelly.

- Place the finely grated courgettes in a sieve and press down to extract as much liquid as possible. Place in a bowl.
- Dry-fry the sesame seeds in a frying pan for 1–2 minutes until they are golden and release their aroma. Add to the courgettes together with the lamb and all the remaining ingredients except the oil and lemon. Season liberally with salt and pepper.
- Form the mixture into 20 small balls and shallow-fry in batches for 5 minutes, turning frequently until evenly browned. Keep the koftas warm in a hot oven while cooking the rest. Serve hot, garnished with lemon wedges.

2 courgettes, finely grated
2 tablespoons sesame seeds
250 g/8 oz minced lamb
2 spring onions, finely chopped
1 garlic clove, crushed
1 tablespoon chopped fresh mint
½ teaspoon ground mixed spice
2 tablespoons dried breadcrumbs
1 egg, lightly beaten
salt and pepper
vegetable oil, for shallow-frying
lemon wedges, to garnish

Serves: 4
Preparation time: 20 minutes
Cooking time: 5 minutes each batch

1 egg, separated

1 tablespoon olive oil

100 ml/3½ fl oz Prosecco or
  sparkling mineral water

65 g/2½ oz plain flour

vegetable oil, for deep-frying

50 g/2 oz sprigs of mixed
  fresh herb leaves, to include
  flat leaf parsley, basil,
  coriander, mint and sage

salt and pepper

salt, to serve

lemon wedges, to garnish

Serves: 4–6
Preparation time: 5 minutes
Cooking time: 30 seconds each

herb fritters

These batter-coated herb sprigs become mouthwateringly tender and succulent as they cook. Try to avoid using rosemary and thyme with very tough stalks. Prosecco is Italian sparking wine which adds a delicate flavour to the batter. Sparkling mineral water can be used instead.

- In a bowl beat together the egg yolk, oil, Prosecco or mineral water and plain flour and season with salt and pepper. Whisk the egg white until stiff and fold into the batter until evenly incorporated.
- In a deep saucepan heat 5 cm/2 inches vegetable oil until it reaches 180–190°C (350–375°F), or until a cube of bread browns in 30 seconds.
- Taking only a few herbs at a time dip the sprigs into the batter and deep-fry for 30 seconds until crisp and golden. Drain on kitchen paper and keep warm in a hot oven while cooking the remaining fritters.
- Serve hot sprinkled with salt and garnished with lemon wedges to squeeze over.

50 g/2 oz sultanas

4 tablespoons Marsala

4 pork escalopes

4 slices Parma ham

16 large sage leaves

125 g/4 oz Fontina cheese, without rind, cut into wafer thin slices

salt and pepper

olive oil, for shallow-frying

1 quantity Salsa Verde, to serve (see page 120)

Serves: 8
Preparation time: 20 minutes, plus soaking time
Cooking time: 10 minutes

pork, Parma ham and sage rolls
with salsa verde

Fontina is an Italian semi-soft cows' milk cheese with a nutty flavour. It melts easily and is similar to mozzarella cheese (which may be used as a substitute).

- Mix the sultanas with the Marsala and set aside to macerate for 1 hour. Drain and pat the sultanas dry.
- Take each pork escalope, place between 2 pieces of baking parchment and pound flat with a mallet or rolling pin. Trim the escalope to an approximate rectangle.
- Top each escalope with a slice of Parma ham, 4 sage leaves, a quarter of the cheese and a quarter of the sultanas. Season with salt and pepper.
- Roll up the escalopes from one long side and skewer with wooden cocktail sticks to secure. Heat a little oil in a frying pan and fry the pork rolls for 10 minutes over a medium heat until browned all over.
- Remove the pork rolls from the frying pan and then leave to cool to room temperature. Remove and discard the cocktail sticks and slice each roll into bite-sized pieces. Spear with clean cocktail sticks and serve with the Salsa Verde.

spicy crab and chicken purses

with sweet and sour dipping sauce

Here squares of filo pastry are stuffed with a Chinese-style chicken and crab filling and baked until crisp and golden. The dipping sauce adds a lovely sweet contrast.

- Place all the ingredients except the filo pastry and oil in a bowl and stir well until combined. Cover and chill for 1 hour to allow the flavours to develop.
- Meanwhile, prepare the dipping sauce. Place all the ingredients in a small saucepan and heat gently, stirring until the sugar is dissolved. Bring to the boil and remove from the heat. Leave until cold and transfer to a small serving bowl.
- Cut the filo pastry into 12 cm/5 inch squares. Brush each one with oil and place a spoonful of the crab and chicken mixture in the centre. Draw the edges up to a point and pinch together. Place the purses on a large greased baking sheet, brush them with oil and bake in a preheated oven, 190°C (375°F), Gas Mark 5, for 20–25 minutes until golden and crisp.
- Serve the purses hot with the dipping sauce.

Makes: 24
Preparation time: 10 minutes, plus chilling time
Cooking time: 20–25 minutes

75 g/6 oz white crab meat, drained if canned

125 g/4 oz cooked chicken, minced

1 garlic clove, crushed

2 spring onions, chopped

1 tablespoon fresh coriander, chopped

2 teaspoons chopped preserved stem ginger, plus 2 teaspoons ginger syrup from the jar

¼ teaspoon chilli powder

1 tablespoon light soy sauce

grated rind and juice of 1 lime

4 filo pastry sheets, defrosted if frozen

4 tablespoons olive oil, plus extra for greasing and brushing

Sweet and Sour Dipping Sauce:

50 g/2 oz sugar

3 tablespoons rice or wine vinegar

½ teaspoon salt

1 teaspoon dried chilli flakes

2 tablespoons water

Serves: 4
Preparation time: 5 minutes
Cooking time: 5 minutes

chorizo sausage
with bread

250 g/8 oz piece mild chorizo
  sausage
3 tablespoons extra virgin
  olive oil
1 garlic clove, sliced
¼ teaspoon dried chilli flakes
2 slices rustic country bread,
  cubed

- Cut the sausage into 5 mm/¼ inch thick slices. Heat the oil in a small frying pan, add the garlic and chilli flakes and fry gently for 30 seconds to 1 minute until they release their aroma. Do not allow them to burn.
- Strain the oil and return to the pan. Add the sausage and stir-fry for 1–2 minutes until golden. Remove with a slotted spoon.
- Toss the bread cubes briefly in the pan juices and drain. Spear a slice of sausage and cube of bread together on cocktail sticks and serve warm.

salt cod *fritters*

250 g/8 oz salt cod
150 ml/¼ pint milk
250 g/8 oz potatoes, cubed
1 garlic clove, crushed
2 spring onions, finely
  chopped
1 tablespoon chopped fresh
  coriander
1 egg yolk
pepper
vegetable oil, for shallow-frying

To Serve:
Skordalia (see page 121) or
  Mayonnaise (see page 125)
lemon wedges

- Put the salt cod into a bowl and cover with cold water. Leave to soak for 24 hours, changing the water several times.
- The following day drain the fish and dry well. Remove the skin and bones and cut into small cubes. Place in a bowl and cover with the milk, leave for 2 hours.
- Drain the cod and place in a pan with the potatoes. Cover with water, bring to the boil and simmer covered, for 20 minutes until the cod and potatoes are tender.
- Drain and mash the fish and potatoes together. Beat in the remaining ingredients, except for the oil and season with pepper.
- Heat about 2.5 cm/1 inch of oil in a deep frying pan. Drop teaspoons of the cod mixture into the oil. Fry for 1–2 minutes until the fritters are browned on all sides.
- Drain on kitchen paper and keep warm in a hot oven while frying the remaining fritters. Serve hot with Skordalia or Mayonnaise to dip and lemon wedges, to squeeze over.

Serves: 8
Preparation time: 35 minutes, plus soaking time
Cooking time: 1–2 minutes each batch

20 large fresh mussels

25 g/1 oz basil leaves

1 garlic clove, crushed

1 small red chilli, deseeded and diced

½ teaspoon grated lemon rind

1 tablespoon pine nuts

1 tablespoon freshly grated Parmesan
  cheese

2 tablespoon fresh breadcrumbs

3–4 tablespoons extra virgin olive oil

salt and pepper

grilled mussels

○ Wash and scrub the mussels pulling out any scraggly beard still attached to the shells. Steam the mussels with just the water on their shells, for 4 minutes until they have just opened. Discard any which do not open. Immediately plunge the mussels into cold water, drain again.

○ Remove the mussels from the pan and carefully discard one half of each shell. Arrange the remaining mussels in 1 large dish or 4 individual gratin dishes.

○ In a blender or food processor combine the basil, garlic, chilli, lemon rind, pine nuts, Parmesan and half of the breadcrumbs. Pulse briefly to form a smooth paste and season to taste with salt and pepper.

○ Transfer the basil paste to a bowl and stir in the oil. Spoon a' little of the paste over each mussel and finally top each one with a few more breadcrumbs. Cook under a preheated grill for 2–3 minutes until bubbling and golden. Serve at once.

Serves: 4
Preparation time: 15 minutes
Cooking time: 2–3 minutes

Several of the recipes in this chapter benefit from cooking over charcoal on the barbecue, particularly the Grilled Sweetcorn with Flavoured Butters, Chicken Saté and Grilled Sweet Potatoes with Coriander and Lemon Salsa. So why not get the barbecue out as soon as the sun arrives?

two bites

cheese stuffed
filo fingers

Makes: 20
Preparation time: 25 minutes
Cooking time: 15–20 minutes

250 g/8 oz Kefalotyri cheese,
  finely grated
250 g/8 oz ricotta cheese
2 eggs, lightly beaten
2 tablespoons chopped fresh
  mint
6 sheets filo pastry
olive oil
2 tablespoons sesame seeds
pepper

Kefalotyri is a hard ewes' milk cheese from Greece. The crumbly texture, pale colour and salty flavour resembles the Sardinian ewes' milk cheese, Pecorino Sardo, which makes a suitable alternative.

- In a bowl beat together the cheeses, eggs and mint and season with black pepper.
- Trim the filo pastry sheets to 20 x 25 cm/8 x 10 inches, if necessary. Then cut each sheet in half lengthways and then crossways to make 24 pieces.
- Working with one piece of pastry at a time (keeping the rest covered with a slightly damp tea towel), brush the pastry with oil.
- Place a little of the filling along one long side and roll up the pastry to enclose the filling. Repeat to make 24 fingers. Place on a lightly oiled large baking sheet.
- Brush the fingers with oil and sprinkle with sesame seeds. Bake in a preheated oven, 200°C (400°F), Gas Mark 6, for 15–20 minutes until golden. Serve at once.

deep-fried
calamari

Serves: 4
Preparation time: 15 minutes
Cooking time: 1–2 minutes each batch

500 g/1 lb small squid, cleaned
vegetable oil, for deep-frying
2 eggs, lightly beaten
2–4 tablespoons flour,
  seasoned with salt, pepper
  and a pinch cayenne pepper

To Serve:
sea salt
lemon juice
1 quantity Aïoli (see page 125)

- Cut the squid into rings and halve the tentacles, if large. Wash well and dry thoroughly on kitchen paper.
- In a deep saucepan heat 5 cm/2 inches vegetable oil until it reaches 180–190°C (350–375°F), or until a cube of bread browns in 30 seconds.
- Meanwhile dip the squid into the beaten egg and coat with the seasoned flour. Deep-fry in batches for 1–2 minutes until crisp and golden. Drain each batch on kitchen paper.
- Keep the cooked squid warm in a hot oven while cooking the remainder. Serve hot sprinkled with sea salt, drizzled with lemon juice and accompanied by a bowl of Aïoli to dip.

15 g/½ oz butter

½ teaspoon sea salt

75 g/3 oz quick cooking polenta

15 g/½ oz freshly grated Parmesan cheese

175 g/6 oz mozzarella cheese

18 large basil leaves

4 tablespoons flour, seasoned with salt and
  pepper

2 eggs, beaten

50 g/2 oz dried plain white breadcrumbs

vegetable oil, for deep-frying

black pepper

Serves: 8
Preparation time: 20 minutes, plus setting and chilling time
Cooking time: 1–2 minutes each batch

polenta triangle sandwiches

These are triangles of set polenta, sandwiched together with mozzarella cheese. They are then coated in breadcrumbs and deep-fried. The mozzarella melts and starts to ooze as it cooks, making a rich and delicious morsel.

- Grease a 20 x 30 cm/8 x 12 inch tin. Bring 900 ml/1½ pints water to a rolling boil, add the butter and salt and then gradually whisk in the polenta in a steady stream.

- Simmer over a low heat for 5–6 minutes, stirring constantly until the mixture comes away from the sides of the pan. Stir in the Parmesan, season with black pepper and pour into the prepared tin. Smooth the surface and set aside to cool.

- Turn the set polenta out and trim to a 15 cm/6 inch square. Cut into 9 x 5 cm/ 2 inch squares and then cut each square in half diagonally, to make 18 triangles.

- Cut the mozzarella into thin slices and then into triangles, roughly the same size as the polenta.

- Place a triangular slice of mozzarella over half the polenta triangles, top with a basil leaf and a piece of polenta. Dip the polenta sandwiches in the seasoned flour, then into the beaten egg and finally in the breadcrumbs to coat well. Chill for 1 hour.

- Heat 5 cm/2 inches vegetable oil in a deep saucepan until it reaches 180–190°C (350–375°F), or until a cube of bread browns in 30 seconds.

- Deep-fry the triangles in batches for 1–2 minutes until crisp and golden. Drain on kitchen paper and keep warm in a hot oven while frying the rest. Serve hot.

Serves: 4
Preparation time: 10 minutes
Cooking time: 6–8 minutes

grilled sweet potatoes

with coriander and lemon salsa

500 g/1 lb sweet potatoes
4 tablespoons olive oil
2 garlic cloves, crushed
salt and pepper

**Coriander and
Lemon Salsa:**

4 tablespoons chopped fresh
  coriander
1 small red chilli, deseeded
  and finely chopped
1 small garlic clove, crushed
6 tablespoons extra virgin
  olive oil
grated rind and juice 1 lemon
½–1 teaspoon ground cumin

○ Scrub the sweet potatoes well but do not peel them. Cut into 5 mm/¼ inch thick slices, pat dry on kitchen paper and place in a large bowl.

○ Mix together the olive oil and garlic and season well with salt and pepper. Pour over the sweet potato slices and toss well to coat.

○ Arrange the potato slices in a single layer on a rack placed over the grill pan. Grill under a preheated grill for 6–8 minutes on each side or until charred and cooked through.

○ Meanwhile, prepare the salsa. Combine all the ingredients in a bowl and season to taste with salt and pepper. Transfer the cooked sweet potato slices to a plate, spoon over the salsa and serve at once.

Serves: 2–4
Preparation time: 18–20 minutes, plus soaking and marinating time
Cooking time: 4–5 minutes

Thai-style
spicy mushroom skewers

You can buy dried shiitake mushrooms from oriental stores where you will find a wide variety of larger shiitake mushrooms. Alternatively, you could dry your own: buy large fresh shiitake and leave them to dry on newspaper for 2–3 days in a warm, dry place, then use as required. This recipe is inspired by a dish cooked by Thai chef, Vatcherin Bhumichitr, in his restaurant Chang Mai.

- Put the dried mushrooms into a bowl and pour over enough boiling water to cover. Leave to soak for 2 hours. Drain the mushrooms and dry thoroughly on kitchen paper. Cut away the tough stalks.
- Using a small pair of scissors cut each mushroom into one long spiral strip starting from the outside and following the shape to the middle.
- Thread the mushroom strips onto bamboo skewers which have been soaked in cold water for 30 minutes, weaving the mushrooms back and forth to zig-zag along the skewers.
- Blend the coriander, garlic, pepper and salt together and stir in the sunflower oil and lemon juice. Spread this mixture all over the mushrooms, cover and leave to marinate for at least 1 hour.
- Place the mushrooms skewers on a rack set over a grill pan, brush with a little oil. Grill under a preheated grill for 4–5 minutes, turning once, until the mushrooms are charred and tender. Serve at once with the Saté Sauce to dip.

16 large dried shiitake mushrooms
2 teaspoons freshly ground coriander
1 garlic clove, crushed
½ teaspoon ground black pepper
½ teaspoon salt
2 tablespoons sunflower oil, plus extra for brushing
2 teaspoons lemon juice
1 quantity Saté Sauce, to serve (see page 50)

Serves: 8
Preparation time: 45 minutes
Cooking time: 1–2 minutes each batch

prawn, rice and pea croquettes

Traditionally these small rice patties were made from leftover paella. They are however, so delicious that they have become a dish in their own right.

15 g/½ oz butter

1 garlic clove, crushed

2 shallots, finely chopped

125 g/4 oz arborio rice

600 ml/1 pint fish or vegetable stock

125 g/4 oz cooked, peeled prawns, roughly chopped

125 g/4 oz frozen peas

2 tablespoons chopped fresh mint

2 tablespoons grated Parmesan cheese

2 eggs, beaten

2–4 tablespoons flour, seasoned with salt and pepper

50 g/2 oz fresh white breadcrumbs

vegetable oil, for deep-frying

salt and pepper

- Melt the butter in a small pan and fry the garlic and shallots for 5 minutes, add the rice and stir-fry for 30 seconds to coat all the grains.
- Add a ladleful of the stock and simmer until reduced. Continue adding stock and stirring the rice for 20 minutes.
- With the final ladle of stock add the prawns and peas, cover and cook for 5–10 minutes until the rice is *al dente* and the peas are cooked.
- Remove the pan from the heat, stir in the chopped mint and grated Parmesan and season to taste with salt and pepper. Cover the surface with greaseproof paper and set aside to cool.
- Once the mixture is cool, beat in half the beaten eggs, 2 tablespoons of seasoned flour and 3 tablespoons of the breadcrumbs. Form into 5 cm/2 inch flat patties, dust with seasoned flour, dip into the remaining beaten egg and finally coat with the remaining breadcrumbs.
- Heat 5 cm/2 inches of oil in a deep saucepan until it reaches 180–190°C (350–375°F), or until a cube of bread browns in 30 seconds.
- Deep-fry the patties in batches for 1–2 minutes until golden, drain on kitchen paper and keep warm in a hot oven while frying the remaining croquettes. Serve at once.

3 small heads sweetcorn

Fennel and Thyme Butter:
1 teaspoon fennel seeds
50 g/2 oz unsalted butter, softened
1 teaspoon chopped fresh thyme
½ teaspoon finely grated lemon rind
1 small garlic clove, crushed
salt and pepper

Chilli and Lime Butter with Sesame:
1 tablespoon sesame seeds
50 g/2 oz unsalted butter, softened
1 small red chilli, deseeded and finely chopped
grated rind and juice ½–1 lime

Serves: 6
Preparation time: 15 minutes, plus chilling time
Cooking time: 10–12 minutes

grilled sweetcorn
with flavoured butters

Use a mallet to help cut through the sweetcorn cobs which tend to be very tough.

○ Start by making the 2 butters. Dry fry the fennel seeds in a small pan until they start to pop and release their aroma. Cool slightly and blend in a spice grinder to form a rough powder.

○ Place all the remaining Fennel and Thyme Butter ingredients in a food processor, add the ground fennel and blend until combined. Season to taste with salt and pepper. Transfer the butter to a piece of foil and roll into a sausage shape. Chill for 30 minutes.

○ For the Chilli and Lime Butter: dry fry the sesame seeds in a small pan until golden. Allow the sesame seeds to cool slightly and place in a food processor with all the remaining ingredients. Season to taste with salt and pepper. Blend until combined. Roll and chill as with the Fennel and Thyme Butter.

○ Using a large sharp knife, cut the sweetcorn into 1 cm/½ inch thick slices and arrange on a rack set over a grill pan.

○ Remove both butters from their foil and cut into thin slices. Top half the sweetcorn slices with one butter and the other half with the remaining butter. Grill under a preheated grill, a good few inches below the heat source, for about 10–12 minutes, turning and adding more butter as required until golden and tender. Serve at once.

2 tablespoons olive oil, plus extra for greasing
250 g (8 oz) chickpea flour
Chilli Oil, for shallow-frying (see page 119)
sea salt and pepper

Serves: 12
Preparation time: 10 minutes, plus setting time
Cooking time: 2–4 minutes

chilli fried panisse

Panisse originates from Nice and is similar to Socca, which is a street food common to Provence; but Socca is sweet and Panisse savoury. Traditionally the fingers are deep-fried, but here I shallow fry them in chilli oil.

- Oil a 23 x 30 cm (9 x 4 inch) tin. Sift the chickpea flour into a bowl. Stir in 1 teaspoon of sea salt and bring 1 litre (1¾ pints) water to a rolling boil. Add the olive oil and then gradually whisk in the water until smooth. Transfer to a non-stick saucepan.
- Bring the mixture to the boil, stirring constantly and cook for 5–6 minutes until thickened and smooth. Transfer the mixture to the prepared tin and leave to cool.
- Turn out of the tin and cut the panisse into fingers. Heat some Chilli Oil in a non-stick frying pan and fry the fingers for 1–2 minutes on each side until golden.
- Season with salt and pepper and serve hot.

Serves: 6
Preparation time: 15 minutes
Cooking time: 1–2 minutes each batch

prawn puffs

12 large raw tiger prawns

vegetable oil, for deep-frying

2 eggs

2 large spring onions, trimmed
   and finely chopped

½ teaspoon Chinese five spice
   powder

2 tablespoons plain flour

salt and pepper

1 quantity Dipping Sauce, to
   serve (see page 67)

- Peel the prawns leaving the tail section intact. Cut down the back of each one and discard the black vein. Wash the prawns and dry thoroughly on kitchen paper.
- Using a sharp knife cut the prawns into 3 slices as far down as the tail section.
- Heat 5 cm/2 inches vegetable oil in a deep saucepan until it reaches 180–190°C (350–375°F), or until a cube of bread browns in 30 seconds.
- In a bowl whisk together the eggs, spring onions, Chinese five spice powder and season with a little salt and pepper. Dip the prawns into the flour and then into the egg mixture.
- Deep-fry the prawns in batches in the hot oil for 1–2 minutes until crisp and golden. Drain on kitchen paper and serve hot with the Dipping Sauce.

chilli chips

Use as little or as much chilli powder as you like, to coat these oven-roasted potato chilli chips.

4 large, even-sized potatoes

4–6 tablespoons olive oil

½ teaspoon salt

1–2 teaspoons chilli powder,
   to taste

soured cream or 1 quantity
   Mayonnaise or Aïoli, to serve
   (see page 125)

- Cut each potato into 8 wedges and place in a large bowl. Add the oil, salt and chilli powder and toss until evenly coated.
- Transfer to a baking sheet and roast in a preheated oven, 220°C (425°F), Gas Mark 7, for 15 minutes. Turn over and cook for a further 15 minutes, turn once more and cook for a final 25–30 minutes until crisp and golden.
- Cool slightly and serve with either soured cream, Mayonnaise or Aïoli.

Serves: 4–6
Preparation time: 5 minutes
Cooking time: 55–60 minutes

Serves: 6
Preparation time: 15 minutes
Cooking time: 2–3 minutes each batch

sesame
prawn toasts

1 spring onion, roughly
  chopped
1 garlic clove, crushed
1 teaspoon grated root ginger
125 g/4 oz cooked peeled
  prawns, well dried
1 tablespoon cornflour
1 teaspoon soy sauce
12 thin slices day old white
  bread
25 g/1 oz sesame seeds
vegetable oil, for deep-frying
lemon wedges, to serve

- Put the spring onion, garlic and ginger in a blender or food processor with the prawns, cornflour and soy sauce and pulse to form a smooth paste.
- Remove the crusts from the bread and spread an even layer of paste over one side. Cut each piece into four triangles and coat with sesame seeds.
- Heat 5 cm/2 inches vegetable oil in a deep saucepan and heat until it reaches 180–190°C (350–375°F), or until a cube of bread browns in 30 seconds.
- Deep-fry the toasts in batches for 2–3 minutes until crisp and golden. Drain on kitchen paper. Serve hot with lemon wedges.

jerk-spiced
fried plantains

2 large ripe plantains
1 tablespoon Jamaican jerk
  spices
2 tablespoons olive oil
25 g/1 oz butter
juice 1 lime
salt

Plantains are available from some supermarkets or from African or Caribbean stores.

- Peel the plantains and cut each one in half crossways. Cut each plantain half into 4 thin slices, dust with the jerk spices.
- Heat the oil and butter together in a large non-stick frying pan. As soon as the butter stops foaming add the plantains to the pan and fry over a medium heat for 3–4 minutes on each side until golden.
- Remove from the pan and drain on kitchen paper. Transfer to a dish and drizzle over the lime juice. Season to taste with salt and serve at once.

Serves: 2–4
Preparation time: 6–8 minutes
Cooking time: 5 minutes

Serves: 4
Preparation time: 5 minutes
Cooking time: 8–10 minutes

grilled mushrooms
with garlic oil

75 ml/3 fl oz extra virgin olive
  oil
2 garlic cloves, crushed
grated rind and juice ½ lime
1 small red chilli, deseeded
  and finely chopped
2 tablespoons chopped fresh
  parsley
12 large flat mushrooms
salt and pepper

Here the mushrooms are grilled first before being dressed with oil, this intensifies the flavour during the cooking process.

- In a small bowl combine all the ingredients except the mushrooms and season to taste with salt and pepper.
- Arrange the mushrooms stalk side down on a foil-lined grill pan and cook under a preheated grill, as close to the heat as possible for 3–4 minutes until beginning to moisten.
- Flip the mushrooms over and cook for a further 4–5 minutes until cooked through. Transfer to a serving plate and pour over the dressing. Leave to cool to room temperature.

12 small oysters, shucked

1 tablespoon red wine vinegar

1 teaspoon Worcestershire sauce

a few drops Tabasco sauce

25 g/1 oz butter

1 shallot, finely chopped

1 garlic clove, crushed

50 g/2 oz piece pancetta or smoked bacon, finely chopped

50 g/2 oz fresh white breadcrumbs

2 tablespoons freshly grated Parmesan cheese

1 tablespoon chopped fresh parsley

a little olive oil

salt and pepper

Serves: 6
Preparation time: 30 minutes
Cooking time: 3–4 minutes

devilled oysters

Your fishmonger will shuck (open) the oysters for you, but ask him to leave the oysters and juices in their shells.

- Carefully strain the juices from the oysters into a bowl and stir in the vinegar, Worcestershire sauce and Tabasco sauce. Cut through the muscle that attaches the oyster to the deep half of the shell, but leave the oysters in the shell. Discard the other half of the shell.
- Melt the butter in a small pan and fry the shallot and garlic for 5 minutes. Add the pancetta or bacon and stir-fry for a further 3–4 minutes until browned.
- Add the breadcrumbs and pour in the oyster juice mixture, boil until the liquid has nearly all evaporated. Remove from the heat and stir in the Parmesan and parsley and season to taste with salt and pepper. Leave to cool.
- Arrange the oysters in a baking dish and top each one with the breadcrumb mixture. Drizzle over a little olive oil and cook under a preheated grill for 3–4 minutes until bubbling and golden. Serve at once.

500 g/1 lb skinless chicken breast fillets

1 small onion, finely chopped

2 teaspoons grated fresh root ginger

2 garlic cloves, crushed

2 tablespoons lime juice

1 tablespoon dark soy sauce

1 tablespoon garam masala

½ teaspoon salt

Saté Sauce:

1 tablespoons groundnut oil

1 garlic clove, crushed

4 tablespoons crunchy peanut butter

¼ teaspoon dried chilli flakes

1 tablespoon dark soy sauce

1 tablespoon lime juice

1 teaspoon clear honey

2 tablespoons coconut cream

Serves: 4– 8
Preparation time: 20 minutes, plus overnight marinating
Cooking time: 4– 6 minutes

chicken saté

Soak the bamboo skewers in cold water for 30 minutes before use. This will prevent them from burning under the grill.

- Cut the chicken breasts on a diagonal into very thin strips and place in a shallow dish. Combine the remaining ingredients for the marinade and pour over the chicken. Stir once, cover and leave to marinate overnight.
- Make the saté sauce. Heat the groundnut oil in a small pan and gently fry the garlic for 2–3 minutes until softened. Stir in the remaining ingredients and heat gently until boiling.
- Drain the chicken and pat dry. Thread the chicken strips onto 8 pre-soaked bamboo skewers, zig-zagging back and forwards as you go. Cook under a preheated grill for 2–3 minutes on each side until charred and cooked through. Serve with the saté sauce, to dip.

24 vine leaves, preserved in brine, drained

4 tablespoons olive oil

I onion, finely chopped

2 garlic cloves, crushed

175 g/6 oz long grain rice

I tablespoon tomato purée

2 teaspoons ground coriander

I teaspoon ground cumin

2 tablespoons chopped fresh dill

I tablespoon chopped fresh mint

25 g/I oz currants

2 tablespoons pine nuts, toasted

4 tablespoons lemon juice

salt and pepper

Mint and Garlic Sauce, to serve (see page 72)

lemon wedges, to garnish

dolmades

- Wash and dry the vine leaves and set aside 16 larger leaves. Use the rest to line a 20 cm/8 inch square baking dish.
- Heat half the oil in a frying pan and fry the onion and garlic for 5 minutes. Add the rice, stir once then add the remaining ingredients, except the lemon juice.
- Lay out the vine leaves, vein side up, and place a spoonful of the filling in the middle of each leaf. Fold the edges around and over the filling, rolling them into a small sausage shape as you go. Repeat to make 16 dolmades.
- Transfer the dolmades to the prepared dish, pour over the remaining oil, the lemon juice and enough water to just cover the parcels. Cover with foil and bake in a preheated oven, 180°C (350°F), Gas Mark 4, for 1 hour.
- Remove from the oven and leave to cool in the dish. Serve warm or cold with Mint and Garlic Sauce and garnished with lemon wedges.

Serves: 8
Preparation time: 30 minutes
Cooking time: I hour

Serves: 4–6
Preparation time: 5 minutes
Cooking time: 5 minutes

fried prawns with garlic butter

12 large raw tiger prawns
2 tablespoons olive oil
50 g/2 oz butter
1 garlic clove, crushed
1 tablespoon chopped fresh
  basil
juice 1 lemon
salt and pepper
Aïoli, to serve (see page 125)

○ Wash and dry the prawns. Heat the oil and butter together in a large frying pan. When the butter stops foaming, add the prawns and crushed garlic and stir-fry for 4–5 minutes until the prawns are pink and golden.

○ Remove the pan from the heat, stir in the basil and squeeze over plenty of lemon juice. Season to taste with salt and pepper. Spoon the prawns into small dishes and serve accompanied with a pot of Aïoli and a finger bowl.

stuffed baby squid

12 baby squid – about
  12 cm/5 inches long, cleaned
5 tablespoons extra virgin
  olive oil
1 small onion, chopped finely
2 garlic cloves, crushed
1 teaspoon chopped fresh
  sage
grated rind and juice ½ lemon
50 g/2 oz fresh white breadcrumbs
25 g/1 oz anchovies, chopped
2 tablespoons chopped fresh
  parsley
25 g/1 oz pine nuts, toasted
  and chopped
50 ml/2 fl oz dry white wine
pepper

Do not over stuff the squid as the filling expands during cooking.

○ Discard the squid tentacles, wash the body cavity of the squid and pat dry on kitchen paper.

○ Heat 1 tablespoon of the oil in a frying pan and fry the onion, garlic, sage and lemon rind for 5 minutes. Transfer to a bowl and stir in the breadcrumbs, anchovies, parsley, pine nuts, lemon juice and plenty of black pepper.

○ Use the mixture to stuff the squid bodies and secure the tops with wooden cocktail sticks. Transfer the stuffed squid to a baking dish, drizzle over the wine and remaining oil and bake in a preheated oven, 230°C (450°F), Gas Mark 8, for 20 minutes. Serve at once.

Serves: 4–6
Preparation time: 25 minutes
Cooking time: 20 minutes

Serves: 4– 6
Preparation time: 10 minutes
Cooking time: 3 minutes each batch

smoked mussel fritters

2 × 85 g/3½ oz cans smoked
  mussels, drained
125 g/4 oz plain flour
1 teaspoon baking powder
1 teaspoon salt
1 small red pepper, seeded
  and finely diced
2 tablespoons chopped fresh
  coriander
½ teaspoon cayenne pepper
1 egg, lightly beaten
65 ml/2½ fl oz beer
1 tablespoon lime juice
vegetable oil, for deep-frying
lime wedges, to serve

Sauce:
4 tablespoon Mayonnaise (see
  page 125)
1 teaspoon wholegrain
  mustard
juice ½ lime
½ teaspoon clear honey

- Roughly chop the mussels and place in a bowl with the flour, baking powder, salt, red pepper, coriander and cayenne and stir well.
- Beat in the egg, beer and lime juice to form a soft dropping batter.
- Heat 5 cm/2 inches vegetable oil in a deep, heavy based saucepan until it reaches 180–190°C (350–375°F), or until a cube of bread browns in 30 seconds.
- Drop the mussel batter, in batches into the hot oil using teaspoon measures, and fry for 3 minutes until golden. Drain on kitchen paper and keep warm in a moderate oven, while cooking the rest.
- Mix all the sauce ingredients together in a bowl. Serve the fritters with the sauce and some lime wedges to squeeze.

Clockwise from far left: Mini Chicken Kievs; Souvlakia; and Piedmontese Peppers

There is a wide selection of interesting snack and starter recipes here, although recipes such as Mini Chicken Kiev, Smoked Salmon and Poached Egg Salad on Muffins and Piedmontese Peppers can all provide simple but satisfying light lunch or supper dishes.

bigger bites

50 g/2 oz unsalted butter, softened

1 garlic clove, crushed

2 teaspoons lemon juice

1 tablespoon chopped fresh parsley

1 tablespoon chopped fresh tarragon

2 large chicken breast fillets, skinned

4 tablespoons flour, seasoned with salt
  and pepper

2 eggs, beaten

125 g/4 oz dried breadcrumbs

salt and pepper

vegetable oil, for shallow-frying

lemon wedges, to garnish

mini chicken kiev

- In a small bowl cream together the butter, garlic, lemon juice and herbs and season with salt and pepper. Form into 4 small blocks, wrap loosely in foil and freeze for 1 hour.
- Take each chicken breast and cut in half horizontally to form 4 escalopes. Flatten each one out by placing between two sheets of baking parchment and tapping firmly with a rolling pin.
- Remove the butter from the freezer and place a block in the middle of each escalope. Fold in half and secure with wooden cocktail sticks.
- Dip each chicken parcel in the seasoned flour, then in the beaten egg and finally in the breadcrumbs to coat thoroughly. Chill for several hours or overnight.
- Heat a shallow layer of oil in a non-stick frying pan and fry the chicken parcels for 15–20 minutes, turning frequently until well browned on all sides. Serve at once, garnished with lemon wedges.

Serves: 4

Preparation time: 25 minutes, plus freezing and chilling time

Cooking time: 15–20 minutes

Serves: 4
Preparation time: 15 minutes
Cooking time: 45 minutes

Piedmontese *peppers*

2 small red peppers

2 large ripe plum tomatoes

2 garlic cloves, sliced

2 tablespoon balsamic vinegar

8 tablespoons extra virgin
olive oil

8 anchovy fillets

4 large basil leaves

salt and pepper

fresh bread, to serve

- Cut each pepper lengthways through the stalk and discard the seeds. Place cut side up in a small roasting pan.
- Peel the tomatoes by immersing them in boiling water for 1 minute. Drain and discard the skin. Cut the tomatoes in half and place one half in each pepper, cut side down.
- Sprinkle the garlic slices over the tomatoes. Combine the vinegar and oil together and drizzle over the tomato-stuffed peppers. Season well with salt and pepper. Pour 2–3 tablespoons of water into the bottom of the tin.
- Bake in a preheated oven, 220°C (425°F), Gas Mark 7, for 30 minutes. Remove from the oven and carefully arrange the anchovy fillets and basil leaves over the tomatoes and bake for a further 15–30 minutes until the peppers are golden and very tender. Cool slightly and serve with the pan juices and bread.

souvlakia

500 g/1 lb neck end of lamb

1 tablespoon chopped fresh
rosemary

2 teaspoons dried oregano

2 teaspoons dried mint

2 bay leaves

1 small onion, chopped

2 garlic cloves, chopped

150 ml/¼ pint red wine

4 tablespoons olive oil

2 pitta breads

50 g/2 oz feta cheese,
crumbled

salt and pepper

Souvlakia is a traditional Greek lamb kebab dish, adapted here to provide a small snack version.

- Cut the lamb into 2.5 cm/1 inch cubes and place in a shallow dish. Combine the herbs, onion, garlic, wine and oil. Season with salt and pepper and pour over the lamb. Stir well, cover and leave to marinate overnight.
- Thread the lamb onto metal skewers and cook over a barbecue or under a preheated grill for 10 minutes, turning and basting frequently. Leave to rest for 5 minutes.
- Grill or toast the pitta bread and cut into quarters. Serve the souvlakia on the pitta scattered with the feta cheese.

Serves: 8
Preparation time: 10 minutes, plus overnight marinating
Cooking time: 10 minutes, plus resting time

8 courgette flowers
8 anchovy fillets

Batter:
1 egg, separated
1 tablespoon olive oil
100 ml/3½ fl oz light beer
65 g/2½ oz plain flour
1 tablespoon chopped fresh basil
salt and pepper
vegetable oil, for deep-frying

Serves: 4 – 8
Preparation time: 10 minutes, plus resting time
Cooking time: 6 – 8 minutes

anchovy stuffed courgette flowers

Even if you do not have a garden, courgettes can be grown in window pots very successfully. Some specialist greengrocers can supply the flowers in season.

- First, make the batter; in a large bowl beat together the egg yolk, oil, beer, flour and basil to make a smooth batter, season with salt and pepper. Cover and set aside for 30 minutes.
- Carefully clean the courgette flowers. Wash and dry the anchovies and slip an anchovy fillet into each flower.
- Heat 5 cm/2 inches vegetable oil in a deep saucepan until it reaches 180–190°C (350–375°F), or until a cube of bread browns in 30 seconds.
- Dip the stuffed flowers into the batter two at a time. Deep-fry in the hot oil for 1–1½ minutes until crisp and golden. Drain on kitchen paper and keep warm in a moderate oven while frying the rest. Serve hot.

Serves: 12
Preparation time: 20 minutes
Cooking time: 15 minutes

chickpea and chard
tortilla

This is a delicious and slightly unusual variation of the more classic potato tortilla. The chickpeas add a lovely nutty flavour to the omelette.

6 tablespoons extra virgin
   olive oil
1 onion, chopped
4 garlic cloves, crushed
½ teaspoon crushed chilli
   flakes
500 g/1 lb chard leaves
1 x 400 g/14 oz can chickpeas,
   drained
6 eggs, beaten
2 tablespoons chopped fresh
   parsley
salt and pepper

- Heat 4 tablespoons of oil in a large non-stick, heavy based frying pan. Add the onion, garlic and chilli flakes and fry gently for 10 minutes until softened and lightly golden.
- Meanwhile, wash and dry the chard and cut away and discard the thick central white stalk. Shred the leaves. Stir the chard into the onion mixture together with the chickpeas and cook gently for 5 minutes.
- Beat the eggs in a bowl and add the parsley and season with salt and pepper. Stir in the chickpea mixture.
- Wipe out the pan, then add the remaining oil. Pour in the egg and chickpea tortilla mixture, cook over a low heat for 10 minutes until the tortilla is almost cooked through.
- Carefully slide the tortilla out onto a large plate, invert the pan over the tortilla and then flip it back into the pan.
- Return the pan to the heat and continue to cook for a further 5 minutes until cooked through. Allow to cool to room temperature and serve cut into squares.

Serves: 8 as an appetizer or 4 as a starter
Preparation time: 10 minutes
Cooking time: 40–45 minutes, plus cooling time

roasted new potatoes

with smoked salmon and caviar filling

16 small new potatoes, about
  40 g/1½ oz each
2 tablespoons olive oil
1 tablespoon chopped fresh
  rosemary
1 tablespoon chopped fresh
  sage
sea salt, for sprinkling
125 g/4 oz crème fraîche
125 g/4 oz smoked salmon,
  cut into strips
25 g/1 oz lumpfish caviar
1 tablespoon snipped fresh
  chives
pepper
lemon wedges, to serve,
  optional

A delicious combination, well worth the time spent assembling.

- Place the potatoes in a roasting tin, add the olive oil, herbs and some sea salt and toss well. Put the roasting tin on the top shelf of a preheated oven, 200°C (400°F), Gas Mark 6, and roast for 40–45 minutes, stirring occasionally, until the potatoes are crisp on the outside and very soft in the centre.

- Remove the potatoes from the oven and leave to cool for 5 minutes. Cut a cross in the top of each potato and press open slightly. Transfer them to a plate and top each with a spoonful of crème fraîche, salmon, caviar and chives. Serve the potatoes at once with plenty of freshly ground black pepper and lemon wedges, if wished.

Serves: 12
Preparation time: 10 minutes
Cooking time: 30 minutes, plus resting time

Spanish tortilla

150 ml/¼ pint extra virgin
   olive oil
750 g/1½ lb potatoes, sliced
   thinly
1 large onion, sliced
5 large eggs, beaten
salt and pepper

This is an authentic Spanish tortilla which is traditionally made with just eggs, potatoes, onions and seasoning and cooked in a large amount of olive oil.

- Heat all but 2 tablespoons of the oil in a 20 cm (8 inch) non-stick frying pan. Add the potato slices and onions and cook, stirring frequently for 15 minutes until the potatoes and onion are golden and tender.
- Stir the potato mixture into the beaten eggs and season generously with salt and pepper. Set aside for 15 minutes. Clean out the frying pan.
- Heat the remaining oil in the clean pan and tip in the tortilla mixture. Cook over a low heat for 10 minutes until almost cooked through. Carefully slide the tortilla onto a large plate, invert the pan over the tortilla and then flip back into the pan.
- Return the pan to the heat and cook for a further 5 minutes or until the tortilla is cooked on both sides. Allow to cool and serve the tortilla at room temperature cut into wedges.

2 large heads garlic
150 ml/¼ pint extra virgin olive oil
2 sprigs fresh rosemary, bruised
salt and pepper

To Serve:
wedge ripe Brie
crusty bread

Serves: 4
Preparation time: 5 minutes
Cooking time: 1¼ hours

baked garlic
with Brie

This classic Californian appetizer can be accompanied by a wedge of Camembert, instead of the Brie. Make sure the cheese is nice and ripe for the best results.

○ Cut a small slice from the top of each head of garlic and sit them in a small baking tin. Pour over half the oil and top with the rosemary sprigs. Season well with salt and pepper, cover with foil and bake in a preheated oven, 200°C (400°F), Gas Mark 6, for 1 hour. Remove the foil, baste and bake for a further 15–20 minutes until caramelized.

○ Split each garlic head in two and then transfer each half to a small plate, drizzle over the remaining oil and serve with a wedge of Brie and plenty of crusty bread.

3 large sole, filleted into
   quarter fillets, skinned,
   washed and dried
4 tablespoons Anchovy Butter
   (see page 106), softened
12 sun-dried tomatoes in oil,
   drained
125 g/4 oz mozzarella cheese,
   cut into 12 dice
olive oil, for greasing
green salad, to serve

Serves: 4
Preparation time: 10 minutes
Cooking time: 8 – 10 minutes

rolled skewered sole fillets
with tomatoes and mozzarella

Here quarter fillets of sole are spread with anchovy butter and rolled up with a sun-dried tomato and a cube of mozzarella. These are then threaded onto skewers and grilled until the fish is cooked and the cheese has melted. You will need 4 skewers.

- Spread the underside of each fish fillet with a little anchovy butter. Place 1 sun-dried tomato and a cube of mozzarella at the narrow end of each fillet. Roll up tightly to enclose the filling and thread 3 rolled fillets on to each skewer. Spread the remaining anchovy butter all over the rolled fish.
- Place the skewers on to a grill pan, lined with foil and greased, and cook under a preheated grill for 8–10 minutes, turning frequently, until the fish is cooked and the cheese in the middle has melted. Serve at once with a crisp green salad.

Thai-style crab cakes *with dipping sauce*

- In a bowl beat together the flour, baking powder, egg, fish sauce, lime juice and chilli sauce until smooth. Stir in the crabmeat, lime leaves and herbs and season with a little salt and pepper. Set aside for 30 minutes to infuse the flavours.
- Meanwhile, prepare the sauce; put the vinegar, sugar, chilli flakes and salt in a small pan and heat gently until the sugar dissolves. Bring to the boil and then remove from the heat to cool.
- Heat a shallow layer of oil in a heavy-based frying pan. Whisk 2 tablespoons of cold water into the crab mixture and drop heaped teaspoons into the oil. Fry for 1 minute on each side until golden.
- Drain on kitchen paper and keep warm in a hot oven while frying the remaining cakes. Serve hot with the dipping sauce.

Serves: 4– 8
Preparation time: 25 minutes, plus infusing time
Cooking time: 2 minutes each batch

65 g/2½ oz plain flour
½ teaspoon baking powder
1 egg, beaten
1 tablespoon Thai fish sauce, (nam pla)
1 tablespoon lime juice
1½ teaspoons chilli sauce
150 g/5 oz crabmeat
4 lime leaves, finely shredded
1 tablespoon chopped fresh coriander
½ tablespoon chopped fresh mint
½ tablespoon chopped fresh basil
salt and pepper
vegetable oil, for shallow-frying

Dipping Sauce:
50 ml/2 fl oz rice vinegar
50 g/2 oz caster sugar
¼ teaspoon crushed chilli flakes
½ teaspoon salt

500 g/1 lb fresh spinach

150 ml/¼ pint extra virgin olive oil

1 onion, finely chopped

4 spring onions chopped

1 garlic cloves, crushed

1 teaspoons dried oregano

2 tablespoons chopped fresh parsley

1 tablespoon chopped fresh dill

2 tablespoons chopped fresh mint

125 g/4 oz ricotta

50 g/2 oz freshly grated Parmesan cheese

1 egg, lightly beaten

12 sheets frozen filo pastry, defrosted

salt and pepper

Serves: 8

Preparation time: 45 minutes

Cooking time: 35–40 minutes, plus cooling time

spanakopita

- Wash the spinach leaves and place them in a large saucepan with just the water clinging to the leaves. Stir over a medium heat for 2–3 minutes until the spinach is wilted. Drain well and squeeze out all the excess liquid. Chop finely.
- Heat 4 tablespoons of the oil in a frying pan and fry the onion, spring onion, garlic and oregano for 10 minutes until softened. Stir in the chopped spinach and fresh herbs and remove from the heat.
- Transfer the mixture to a bowl and stir in the ricotta, Parmesan and the egg. Season with salt and pepper and mix until evenly combined.
- Take one sheet of filo pastry and brush with oil, place in an oiled 20 x 25 cm (8 x 10 inch) baking tin. Repeat with a further 5 sheets of pastry. Spread the filling over the pastry and top with the remaining sheets of pastry, brushing with oil as you go.
- Using a sharp knife score the top of the pie with a diamond pattern cutting down as far as the filling. Brush over any remaining oil and bake in a preheated oven, 190°C (375°F), Gas Mark 5, for 35–40 minutes until the pastry is golden. Allow to cool for 10 minutes, then cut into squares and serve warm.

Serves: 4
Preparation time: 20 minutes, plus soaking time
Cooking time: 25–30 minutes

bulghar stuffed **tomatoes**

50 g/2 oz bulghar wheat

4 beef tomatoes

2 tablespoons olive oil, plus extra for drizzling

1 onion, finely chopped

2 tablespoons pine nuts

2 garlic cloves, crushed

1 teaspoon ground cumin

2 tablespoons raisins

2 tablespoons chopped fresh parsley

1 tablespoon chopped fresh mint

125 g/4 oz Cheddar cheese, grated

salt and pepper

- Soak the bulghar in plenty of hot water for 30 minutes, drain well and squeeze out the excess liquid.
- Cut a thin slice from the top of each tomato, discard the seeds, then scoop out and finely chop the flesh.
- Heat the oil in a frying pan and fry the onion, pine nuts, crushed garlic and cumin for 10 minutes until softened. Stir in the bulghar and the tomato pulp and fry for a further 5 minutes.
- Remove the pan from the heat and stir in the raisins, parsley, mint and half the cheese and season to taste with salt and pepper. Spoon the mixture into the empty tomato shells and scatter over the remaining cheese.
- Transfer the tomatoes to a small baking dish, drizzle over a little extra oil and bake in a preheated oven, 190°C (375°F), Gas Mark 5, for 25–30 minutes until the tomatoes are very soft and the cheese crisp and golden.

spare ribs

Cooking the ribs in water and vinegar tenderizes the meat so that when cooked, the meat literally melts in the mouth.

500 g/1 lb pork spare ribs

1 tablespoon distilled malt vinegar

1 tablespoon sesame oil

50 ml/2 fl oz white wine vinegar

2 tablespoons dark soy sauce

1 tablespoon tomato ketchup

1 garlic clove, crushed

1 teaspoon freshly grated root ginger

2 tablespoons clear honey

¼ teaspoon Chinese five spice powder

pinch of chilli powder

- Place the spare ribs in a saucepan, add the malt vinegar and enough water to cover. Bring to the boil, skimming the surface and simmer for 20 minutes.
- Drain the ribs and transfer to a roasting tin. Meanwhile place all the remaining ingredients in a small pan with 50 ml/2 fl oz water and bring to the boil. Pour over the ribs and toss well to coat.
- Cover the roasting tin with foil and bake in a preheated oven, 220°C (425°F), Gas Mark 7, for 30 minutes. Remove the foil, baste the ribs by stirring once. Return to the oven and cook for a further 30 minutes, basting occasionally until tender. Cool slightly and serve with a finger bowl.

Serves: 4
Preparation time: 25 minutes
Cooking time: 1 hour

1 tablespoon groundnut oil

125 g/4 oz minced pork

½ teaspoon crushed chilli flakes

½ tablespoon dark soy sauce

½ tablespoon soft dark brown sugar

½ tablespoon dry sherry

1 tablespoon white wine vinegar

50 g/2 oz creamed coconut, chopped

50 g/2 oz bean sprouts

2 tablespoons chopped fresh coriander

6 large chicory leaves

salt and pepper

coriander sprigs, to garnish

Serves: 6
Preparation time: 5 minutes
Cooking time: 15 – 20 minutes

sweet and sour minced pork

- Heat the oil in a frying pan and stir-fry the pork and chilli flakes for 5 minutes until the pork is browned. Add the soy sauce, sugar and sherry and stir-fry for a further 1 minute.
- Stir in the vinegar and coconut and 2–3 tablespoons water until blended and then simmer gently for 10 minutes. Remove from the heat and stir in the bean sprouts and coriander, then season to taste with salt and pepper.
- Pile the pork mixture into the chicory leaves, garnish with coriander sprigs and serve immediately.

Serves: 4
Preparation time: 10 minutes, plus marinating time
Cooking time: 6–8 minutes

spicy grilled lamb cutlets

8 small lamb cutlets

2 teaspoons paprika

¼ teaspoon cayenne pepper

1 tablespoon sesame seeds

1 tablespoon chopped fresh
  thyme

2 tablespoons olive oil

1 tablespoon lemon juice

salt and pepper

Mint and Garlic Sauce:

125 g/4 oz Greek yogurt

1 garlic clove, crushed

2 tablespoons chopped fresh
  mint

pinch of sugar

- Trim the cutlets of excess fat and place in a shallow dish. Place the paprika, cayenne, sesame seeds and thyme in a spice grinder or a pestle and mortar and blend to a powder. Transfer to a dish and stir in the oil, lemon juice and a little salt and pepper.
- Pour over the lamb and rub well into the meat. Cover and marinate for several hours or overnight. Remove from the refrigerator at least 1 hour before cooking.
- Prepare the sauce. In a bowl mix all the ingredients together until combined and season with salt and pepper to taste, set aside until required.
- Place the marinated cutlets on a rack, set over the grill pan and grill under a preheated grill for 3–4 minutes on each side until golden and cooked through.
- Allow the cutlets to cool slightly and serve with the Mint and Garlic Sauce to dip.

spiced lamb kebabs

500 g/1 lb minced lamb

1 tablespoon lemon juice

1 small onion, minced

2 garlic cloves, crushed

1 teaspoon grated root ginger

2 tablespoons chopped fresh
  parsley

1 tablespoon chopped fresh
  mint

2 teaspoons ground coriander

1 teaspoon ground turmeric

1 teaspoon ground cumin

1 teaspoon ground cinnamon

1 tablespoon chilli sauce

1 egg, beaten

salt and pepper

Greek Yogurt or Aïoli (see
  page 125), to serve

Soaking the bamboo skewers in cold water for 30 minutes before use stops them from burning under the grill.

- Combine all the ingredients except the egg in a large bowl until evenly blended. Season with salt and pepper. Cover and leave to infuse for at least 1 hour.
- Soak 16 bamboo skewers in cold water for 30 minutes and pat dry. Stir the egg into the lamb and mix well. Divide the meat mixture into 16 and shape into small sausages.
- Thread one sausage shape onto each skewer. Cook over a barbecue or on a wire rack under a preheated grill for 10 minutes, turning from time to time until browned and cooked through. Cool slightly and serve the lamb with Greek yogurt or Aïoli.

Serves: 8
Preparation time: 10 minutes, plus marinating time
Cooking time: 10 minutes

Serves: 8
Preparation time: 40 minutes
Cooking time: 15 – 20 minutes

salmon and potato parcels

250 g/8 oz potatoes, peeled

15 g/½ oz butter

½ onion, finely chopped

¼ teaspoon fennel seeds, roughly ground

1 teaspoon finely grated lemon rind

1 tablespoon chopped fresh dill

75 g/6 oz smoked salmon, finely chopped

1 tablespoon lemon juice

1 egg yolk

500 g/1 lb puff pastry, defrosted if frozen

salt and pepper

Egg Glaze:

1 small egg

1 tablespoon milk

○ Cook the potatoes in lightly salted boiling water for about 15 minutes until cooked. Drain well and mash with a fork (the texture of the potato mash should remain fairly rough).

○ Melt the butter in a small pan and fry the onion, fennel and lemon rind for 10 minutes until very soft. Transfer to a bowl and stir in the mashed potato, dill, salmon, lemon juice and egg yolk until well blended, season with salt and pepper. Roll out the pastry to form a thin rectangle 18 x 35 cm/7 x 14 inches and cut into 6 squares measuring 8.5 cm/3½ inches.

○ Divide the filling between the squares, placing a mound slightly off centre. Dampen the edges of the pastry and fold each one in half diagonally to form a triangle. Press together to seal.

○ Transfer the triangles to a lightly greased baking sheet. Beat the ingredients for the egg glaze together and season with a pinch of salt. Brush the glaze lightly over the pastry. Bake in a preheated oven, 220°C (425°F), Gas Mark 7, for 15–20 minutes until puffed up and golden. Serve hot.

Makes: 14
Preparation time: 45 minutes, plus rising and soaking time
Cooking time: 15–20 minutes, plus cooling time

piroshki

Piroshki (or pirozhki) is the Russian name given to these small stuffed bread parcels. The stuffing can be made using meat or fish as well as a vegetable mixture.

Dough:

250 g/8 oz plain flour

½ teaspoon salt

2 teaspoons fast-acting dried yeast

1 teaspoon sugar

50–75 ml/2–3 fl oz warm milk

1 small egg, beaten

25 g/1 oz melted butter

Filling:

15 g/½ oz dried ceps

25 g/1 oz butter

4 large spring onions, finely chopped

2 garlic cloves, crushed

250 g/8 oz chestnut mushrooms, finely chopped

2 tablespoons chopped fresh dill

50 g/2 oz cooked rice

2 hard boiled eggs, finely chopped

2 tablespoons soured cream

salt and pepper

1 quantity Egg Glaze (see page 73)

- Start by making the dough. Sift the flour and salt into the bowl of a food mixer and stir in the yeast and sugar. With the dough hook on a low setting gradually blend in the milk, egg and melted butter to form a soft, slightly sticky dough. Knead for 10 minutes.
- If you wish to make the dough by hand, sift the flour and salt into a bowl and stir in the fast-acting yeast. Make a well in the centre and gradually work in the milk, egg and butter to form a soft, slightly sticky dough. Turn out and knead on a lightly floured surface for 10 minutes until the dough is smooth and elastic.
- Cover the bowl with cling film and leave to rise in a warm place until doubled in size, about 1½–2 hours.
- Put the dried ceps into a bowl, add 150 ml/¼ pint boiling water and set aside to soak for 30 minutes. Drain and reserve the liquid, chop and reserve the ceps.
- Melt the butter in a frying pan and fry the spring onions and garlic for 5 minutes. Add the ceps and chestnut mushrooms and continue to fry over a high heat for 5–6 minutes until the mushrooms are golden.
- Add the reserved cep liquid and boil until it has almost evaporated. Transfer to a bowl and stir in the remaining ingredients, except the egg glaze. Season with salt and pepper to taste. Set aside to cool.
- Knock back the dough and then divide into 14 balls. Roll each one out on a lightly floured surface to a 10 cm/4 inch round.
- Take a spoonful of the mushroom filling and place in the centre of each round. Brush the edges with a little egg glaze, pull up the sides and pinch together across the centre to seal in the filling (like a Cornish pasty).
- Transfer the piroshki to lightly greased baking sheets, cover loosely with greased cling film and leave to rise for a further 20–30 minutes.
- Bake in a preheated oven, 200°C (400°F), Gas Mark 6, for 15–20 minutes until risen and golden. Allow to cool for about 10 minutes. Serve warm.

smoked salmon and poached egg salad *on muffins*

1 tablespoon distilled white
   vinegar
4 eggs
2 plain muffins, halved
25 g/1 oz Anchovy Butter
   (see page 106)
125 g/4 oz frisé lettuce
250 g/8 oz smoked salmon
1 tablespoon poppy seeds
snipped fresh chives,
   to garnish

Dressing:

2 teaspoons champagne or
   white wine vinegar
1 teaspoon Dijon mustard
1 tablespoon snipped fresh
   chives
6 tablespoons extra virgin
   olive oil
2 ripe tomatoes, skinned,
   deseeded and diced
salt and pepper

For hard poached eggs follow the instructions below but cook the eggs in the water for 3–4 minutes.

○ First poach the eggs. Bring a small frying pan of water to a gentle simmer, add the vinegar and then carefully break in the eggs to fit closely together. Remove the pan from the heat and leave the eggs in the water to poach until just set.

○ Meanwhile, grill both sides of the muffins under a preheated grill until golden; split and spread the insides with anchovy butter and return to the grill for a further 1–2 minutes until golden.

○ Blend together all the dressing ingredients except the tomatoes, taste and adjust the seasoning, if necessary and toss half with the frisé lettuce. Stir the diced tomato into the remaining dressing.

○ Arrange the muffins on serving plates, top each with the smoked salmon, the dressed frisé and sprinkle over the poppy seeds. Carefully remove the poached eggs from the water with a slotted spoon, drain on kitchen paper and place 1 egg on top of each muffin. Pour the tomato dressing around each muffin and serve at once, garnished with the snipped chives.

Serves: 4
Preparation time: 20 minutes
Cooking time: 10 minutes

Clockwise from far left: Seafood Escabèche; Potato Bravas; Butterfly Chilli Prawns; and Broad Beans with Serrano Ham

little dishes

Why not prepare around six of the dishes in the following chapter and arrange them in pretty coloured bowls in the centre of your dinner table? Supply large plates and plenty of napkins and get your guests to help themselves.

Serves: 4–6
Preparation time: 20–25 minutes, plus marinating time
Cooking time: 3 minutes

butterfly **chilli prawns**

12 large raw Mediterranean
prawns, about 500 g/1 lb
4 tablespoons extra virgin
olive oil, plus extra to serve
4 garlic cloves, sliced
½ teaspoon crushed chilli
flakes
grated rind and juice 1 lemon
salt and pepper
4 tablespoons chopped fresh
parsley, to garnish

To Serve:
lemon wedges
fresh bread

- Using a sharp serrated knife cut down the back of the prawns through the shell, but do not cut completely in half. Pull out and discard the black vein and wash and dry the prawns. Butterfly the prawns out by turning them flesh side down and pressing flat.
- Combine the olive oil, garlic, chilli flakes, lemon rind and juice and season with a little salt and pepper. Place the prawns in a large tray, pour over the oil mixture, cover and chill for 2 hours.
- Heat a large iron griddle or heavy-based frying pan. Place the prawns shell side down on the hot pan in a single layer and cook for 1–2 minutes until the shells shrivel and the flesh starts to turn pink. Flip the prawns and cook for a further 30 seconds.
- Transfer the prawns to a serving dish, garnish with the parsley and drizzle over some more olive oil. Serve with lemon wedges and fresh bread.

broad beans
with Serrano ham

1 tablespoon olive oil
125 g/4 oz piece Serrano ham,
diced
2 garlic cloves, sliced
250 g/8 oz freshly podded
broad beans – 750 g/1½ lb in
the pod
75 ml/3 fl oz dry white wine
2 tomatoes, peeled, deseeded
and diced
1 tablespoon chopped
fresh dill
salt and pepper

Serrano ham is a Spanish cured ham similar to the Italian Parma ham, which can be substituted. You will need to ask for the ham to be cut into one thick slice for this dish.

- Heat the oil in a frying pan, add the ham and fry briefly to brown on all sides. Lower the heat, add the garlic and broad beans and fry gently for 5 minutes.
- Add the wine and diced tomatoes, bring to the boil, cover and simmer for 10–15 minutes until the beans are tender. Season to taste with salt and pepper, stir in the dill and serve at once.

Serves: 4
Preparation time: 12 minutes
Cooking time: 15–20 minutes

Serves: 4
Preparation time: 25 – 30 minutes, plus chilling and resting time
Cooking time: 15 minutes

seafood **escabèche**

16 large mussels, scrubbed
250 g/8 oz baby squid, cleaned
250 g/8 oz peeled small raw
  Mediterranean prawns,
  de-veined (see page 79)
2 garlic cloves, chopped
1 small red chilli, deseeded
  and chopped
50 ml/2 fl oz dry sherry
1 tablespoon chopped basil,
  to garnish
bread, to serve

Marinade:
150 ml/¼ pint extra virgin
  olive oil
2 shallots, chopped
3 tablespoons white wine
  vinegar
pinch of sugar
1 tablespoon drained and
  chopped capers in brine
salt and pepper

Escabèche means 'marinated' and is a classic Spanish tapas dish. Other fish or even vegetables can be used as well as seafood.

- Prepare the seafood; remove any beard still attached to the mussels. Cut the squid into rings and the tentacles in half, if large, wash well. Wash and dry the raw prawns.
- Put the mussels into a pan with the garlic, chilli and sherry, cover and steam for 4–5 minutes until all the mussels are opened (discard any that remain closed). Remove the mussels with a slotted spoon and set aside.
- Poach the prawns in the mussel liquid for 4–5 minutes until cooked. Poach the squid for 2–3 minutes until cooked. Remove with a slotted spoon and add to the mussels. Reserve 2 tablespoons of the cooking liquid and leave to cool.
- Combine all the marinade ingredients and stir in the reserved poaching liquid. Pour over the cold seafood, toss well and chill for several hours.
- Return the escabèche to room temperature for 1 hour, scatter over the basil and serve with bread.

potato bravas

1 kg/2 lb small potatoes
2 tablespoons olive oil
sea salt

Sauce:
4 tablespoons olive oil
1 tablespoon tomato purée
1 tablespoon red wine vinegar
1 teaspoon chilli sauce
2 teaspoons paprika
salt and pepper

- Cut the potatoes into 1 cm/½ inch thick slices and place in a single layer on a baking sheet.
- Brush with olive oil, sprinkle with sea salt and roast in a preheated oven, 230°C (450°F), Gas Mark 8, for 20 minutes. Turn the potatoes over and bake for a further 10 minutes until crisp and golden.
- Combine the sauce ingredients with 2 tablespoons water in a sauté pan. Add the cooked potatoes, heat through, season to taste with salt and pepper and serve hot.

Serves: 4
Preparation time: 5 minutes
Cooking time: 30 minutes

Serves: 4
Preparation time: 10 minutes, plus marinating time
Cooking time: 5 minutes

chilli scallops

8 large scallops in their shells
2 tablespoons sunflower oil,
   plus extra for frying
1 teaspoon sesame oil
1 tablespoon dark soy sauce
1 teaspoon grated root ginger
pinch Chinese five spice
   powder
1 tablespoon Thai red curry
   paste
1 tablespoon chopped fresh
   coriander
1–2 tablespoons sesame
   seeds
150 ml/¼ pint fish or
   vegetable stock

To Garnish:
coriander sprigs
2 red chillies, sliced

You can use ready shelled scallops for this dish, just serve the cooked scallops in small dishes rather than their shells.

- Carefully remove the scallops from their shells by snipping through the muscle that attaches them (or ask your fishmonger to clean the scallops for you). Wash and reserve the deep shells, wash and dry the scallops discarding the muscle.
- Combine the remaining ingredients, except the sesame seeds and stock, in a shallow dish. Add the scallops, toss well to coat and leave to marinate for at least 1 hour.
- Remove the scallops from their marinade and coat with the sesame seeds. Scrape the marinade into a pan and add the stock. Simmer until reduced by half.
- Heat a little oil on a griddle or in a heavy-based frying pan. When very hot add the scallops and fry for 1 minute on each side. Serve the scallops either in their shells or in small dishes. Pour the marinade over the scallops and garnish with coriander and chillies.

Serves: 4–6
Preparation time: 20 minutes, plus overnight soaking
Cooking time: 15 minutes

brandade of **salt cod**

175 g/6 oz salt cod
150 ml/¼ pint olive oil
150 ml/¼ pint full fat milk (or
  milk and cream mixed)
2 large garlic cloves, crushed
2 tablespoons chopped fresh
  chives
1 teaspoon lemon juice
pepper

To Serve:
vegetable crudités
French bread

Salt cod is available from good fishmongers or Mediterranean food shops. It needs to be soaked in several changes of cold water for 24 hours before cooking.

- Place the salt cod in a large bowl and cover with cold water. Leave to soak for 24 hours changing the water several times if possible.
- Drain the cod, rinse well and place in a saucepan. Add enough cold water to cover, bring to the boil and poach gently for 10 minutes. Drain, cool and dry well. Discard the bones and skin and flake the flesh.
- Place the oil, milk and garlic in a saucepan and heat gently until the mixture just begins to boil.
- Put the fish into a blender or food processor and pulse briefly. Then with the blade running, gradually pour in the oil mixture through the funnel until a smooth creamy paste is made.
- Transfer the brandade to a bowl, stir in the chives, add the lemon juice and season with black pepper. Serve the brandade with a selection of fresh vegetable crudités and some French bread.

Serves: 4
Preparation time: 10 minutes, plus marinating time

Moroccan carrot salad

500 g/1 lb carrots
1 garlic clove, crushed
1 teaspoon salt
pinch of sugar
6 tablespoons extra virgin
  olive oil
2 tablespoons red wine
  vinegar
½ teaspoon ground cumin
¼ teaspoon cayenne pepper
1 tablespoon chopped fresh
  coriander
pepper

- Using the grater attachment of the food processor (or the finest side of a box grater) thinly grate the carrots. Transfer to a sieve and drain off any excess liquid.
- Combine all the remaining ingredients adjusting the seasoning to taste. Stir into the grated carrot, cover and leave to marinate in the refrigerator for at least 1 hour. Serve slightly chilled.

cauliflower with anchovy and garlic sauce

1 large head cauliflower,
  trimmed
25 g/1 oz anchovy fillets
½ quantity Aïoli (see
  page 125)
pepper
1 tablespoon chopped fresh
  parsley, to garnish

- Cut the cauliflower into large florets and steam for 10–12 minutes until tender. Transfer to a large shallow dish with 1 tablespoon of the cooking liquid.
- Finely chop the anchovy fillets and stir into the Aïoli. Pour the Aïoli over the cauliflower florets while still warm and toss to coat. Season with a little black pepper and garnish with chopped parsley. Serve warm.

Serves: 8
Preparation time: 5–6 minutes
Cooking time: 10–12 minutes

Serves: 6
Preparation time: 5 minutes, plus overnight soaking
Cooking time: 2 hours

large butter beans *in tomato sauce*

250 g/8 oz dried butter beans,
  soaked overnight in cold
  water
2 × 400 g/14 oz cans chopped
  tomatoes
300 ml/½ pint vegetable stock
2 garlic cloves, chopped
2 tablespoons extra virgin
  olive oil
1 tablespoon chopped fresh
  oregano
2 bay leaves
1 teaspoon caster sugar
1 tablespoon lemon juice
2 tablespoons chopped
  fresh dill
salt and pepper

This is a classic Greek dish known as Gigantes Plaki *and can be found in tavernas throughout Greece, where they are served as part of a mezze.*

○ Drain the soaked beans, wash well and set aside. Put the tomatoes, stock, garlic, olive oil, oregano, bay leaves and sugar in a large saucepan and bring to the boil. Stir in the beans, return to the boil, cover and simmer over a low heat for 1½ hours or until the beans are very tender. Remove the lid and simmer for a further 30 minutes until the sauce is reduced and thickened.

○ Stir in the lemon juice, chopped dill and season with salt and pepper, leave to cool slightly. Serve warm with some crusty bread.

Serves: 4
Preparation time: 10 minutes
Cooking time: 4–6 minutes each

grilled Mediterranean vegetables

1 small aubergine

1 large courgette

1 red pepper, deseeded

1 red onion

3 garlic cloves

1 teaspoon cumin seeds

1 tablespoon chopped fresh
 thyme

1 tablespoon balsamic vinegar

150 ml/¼ pint extra virgin
 olive oil

salt and pepper

1 tablespoon chopped fresh
 basil

- First prepare the vegetables. Cut the aubergine into 8 slices; the courgette into 5 mm/¼ inch thick diagonal slices; the pepper into thick strips and the onion into thick wedges. Place in a large bowl.

- In a spice grinder or a pestle and mortar, mash the garlic, cumin seeds and thyme to a paste and stir in the balsamic vinegar, 125 ml/4 fl oz of the oil and season with salt and pepper. Pour over the vegetables and toss well to coat.

- Grill the vegetables under a preheated grill a few at a time for 2–3 minutes on each side until charred and tender.

- Transfer the vegetables to a warmed serving plate, drizzle over the remaining olive oil and scatter over the basil. Serve warm.

2 large herrings, filleted

juice 2 lemons

125 g/4 oz crème fraîche

1 tablespoon hot horseradish sauce

salt and pepper

1 tablespoon chopped fresh dill, to garnish

Marinade:

150 ml/¼ pint white wine vinegar

75 g/3 oz caster sugar

1 garlic clove, sliced

1 small red onion, sliced

2 bay leaves

2 sprigs fresh dill, bruised

1 teaspoon all spice berries, bruised

6 white peppercorns

Serves: 4

Preparation time: 25 minutes, plus marinating and resting time

marinated herring
with horseradish cream

- Using a pair of tweezers pull out as many of the tiny bones from the herring fillets as possible. Wash and dry well. Place the fillets skin side down in a ceramic dish and pour over the lemon juice. Cover and chill for 2 hours.
- Meanwhile, prepare the marinade. Combine all the ingredients in a bowl with 150 ml/¼ pint cold water and set aside. Stir occasionally to dissolve the sugar.
- Drain the herrings and discard the juices. Cut the fish into bite-sized pieces, return to the dish and pour over the marinade. Cover and leave to marinate overnight in the fridge.
- Remove the herring fillets from the marinade and allow them to return to room temperature for 1 hour. Discard the marinade.
- Combine the crème fraîche and horseradish sauce in a small bowl and season with a little salt and pepper to taste.
- Arrange the herrings on a platter with the bowl of horseradish cream and garnish with chopped fresh dill.

Serves: 8
Preparation time: 10 minutes
Cooking time: 8–10 minutes,

pasta with
herb sauce

250 g/8 oz dried pasta

100 ml/3½ fl oz extra virgin
   olive oil, plus extra to serve

grated rind and juice 1 small
   lemon

1 garlic clove, crushed

25 g/1 oz fresh herbs; to
   include basil, chervil, chives,
   dill and parsley

4 anchovy fillets in oil, drained
   and chopped

1 tablespoon chopped capers
   in brine, drained

salt and pepper

- Bring a large pan of lightly salted water to a rolling boil, add the pasta, return to the boil and cook for 8–10 minutes until *al dente*.
- Meanwhile place all the remaining ingredients in a blender or food processor and blend to form a smooth sauce. Season to taste with salt and pepper.
- Strain the pasta, reserving 2 tablespoons of the cooking water. Toss the pasta with the herb sauce, adding the reserved cooking liquid. Leave to cool to room temperature, taste and adjust the seasoning; add a little extra olive oil if necessary.

Serves: 4
Preparation time: 15 minutes
Cooking time: 10 minutes

kidneys cooked with sherry

8 veal or lamb kidneys
juice 1 lemon
2 tablespoons olive oil
1 garlic clove, crushed
125 g/4 oz pancetta, chopped
50 ml/2 fl oz dry sherry
2 tablespoons chopped fresh
  parsley
salt and pepper

○ Halve the kidneys and cut out the white cores. Place the kidneys in a bowl, add the lemon juice and set aside for 10 minutes.

○ Heat the oil in a frying pan and when hot add the kidneys, garlic and pancetta and stir over a high heat for 3–4 minutes until browned.

○ Add the sherry and simmer for a further 3–4 minutes until the sherry is reduced and the kidneys cooked through. Sprinkle over the parsley, season to taste with salt and pepper and serve at once.

Serves: 4
Preparation time: 5 minutes
Cooking time: 15–20 minutes

roasted vine tomatoes

with goats' cheese

500 g/1 lb cherry tomatoes
  on the vine

2 garlic cloves, sliced

2 sprigs fresh thyme

6 tablespoons extra virgin
  olive oil

175 g/6 oz fresh goats' cheese

salt and pepper

toast, to serve

○ Place the tomatoes still attached to the vine in a shallow roasting tin. Scatter over the garlic and thyme and drizzle over the oil.

○ Place in a preheated oven, 230°C (450°F), Gas Mark 9 for 15–20 minutes until browned and softened. Spoon the tomatoes on to toasted bread, top with the goats' cheese and pour over the pan juices. Serve immediately.

Serves: 4
Preparation time: 25 – 30 minutes, plus overnight chilling
Cooking time: 20 minutes

chicken liver pâté
with sweet and sour onion salsa

250 g/8 oz chicken livers
1 shallot, finely chopped
50 g/2 oz butter
3 tablespoons Madeira
3 tablespoons double cream
1 teaspoon pink peppercorns,
   crushed
salt and pepper
crisp bread or toast, to serve

Sweet and Sour Onion Salsa:

2 red onions, sliced
1 tablespoon olive oil
3 tablespoons balsamic vinegar
2 tablespoons soft brown
   sugar
1 sprig fresh rosemary, bruised

The onion salsa with its sweet and sour flavour cuts through the rich creaminess of the pâté, making it a perfect partner. To bruise the rosemary, lightly crush it with a rolling pin, this will help to release its flavour into the salsa.

- Trim the chicken livers discarding any discoloured parts, wash and dry well. Fry the shallot in the butter for 5 minutes.
- Increase the heat and add the chicken livers. Fry for 3–4 minutes until browned on all sides, but still slightly pink in the centre.
- Remove the livers using a slotted spoon and place in a blender. Add the Madeira to the frying pan and reduce by half, scraping the sediment from the base.
- Scrape into the blender and add the cream and a little salt. Purée to form a smooth paste and pass through a fine sieve, stir in the peppercorns and spoon into a small dish. Leave to cool and then chill overnight.
- Make the salsa. Place all the ingredients in a saucepan with 4 tablespoons water and season with salt and pepper. Simmer over a low heat for 20 minutes until soft and caramelized. Leave to cool. Serve the pâté and salsa together with some crisp bread or toast.

Serves: 2–4
Preparation time: 5 minutes
Cooking time: 15 minutes

haricot beans
with lemon, rosemary and chilli

2 tablespoons extra virgin
  olive oil, plus extra to serve
1 small onion, finely chopped
2 garlic cloves, chopped
1 red chilli, deseeded and
  diced
1 teaspoon chopped fresh
  rosemary
grated rind and juice ½ lemon
1 x 400 g/14 oz can haricot
  beans, drained
1 tablespoon chopped fresh
  parsley
salt and pepper

- Heat the oil in a frying pan and fry the onion, garlic, chilli, rosemary and lemon rind for 10 minutes until softened but not browned.
- Stir in the haricot beans, lemon juice and 2 tablespoons of water, bring to the boil, cover and simmer gently for 5 minutes.
- Remove from the heat, season to taste with salt and pepper and leave to cool. Stir in the parsley and serve the beans drizzled with olive oil.

Pacific Rim mussels

2 tablespoons vegetable oil
1 small onion, finely chopped
2 garlic cloves, crushed
1 teaspoon grated root ginger
1 teaspoon hot curry paste
¼ teaspoon ground allspice
pinch cayenne pepper
1 x 400 g/14 oz can chopped
  tomatoes
2 lime leaves, shredded
750 g/1½ lb large fresh
  mussels, scrubbed and
  cleaned, beards removed
salt and pepper
1 tablespoon chopped fresh
  coriander, to garnish

- Heat the oil in the bottom of a double boiler or large saucepan. Add the onion, garlic, ginger, curry paste and spices and fry gently for 10 minutes until softened.
- Add the chopped tomatoes and shredded lime leaves, cover and simmer for 20 minutes until thickened. Season to taste with salt and pepper.
- Place the mussels either in the top of the double-boiler, or in a steamer set over the saucepan. Steam the mussels over the sauce for 5 minutes. Discard any mussels which do not open.
- Carefully discard one half of each mussel shell and arrange the mussels in individual serving dishes. Spoon over the sauce and serve at once garnished with the chopped coriander.

Serves: 6
Preparation time: 25 minutes
Cooking time: 5–10 minutes

½ cucumber, peeled, halved and deseeded

50 g/2 oz vermicelli rice noodles

1 carrot, cut into long julienne strips

1 red chilli, deseeded and cut into long julienne strips

2 tablespoons chopped fresh coriander

salt

coriander sprigs, to garnish

Dressing:

2 tablespoons sunflower oil

½ teaspoon sesame oil

2 teaspoons caster sugar

2 tablespoons lime juice

1 tablespoon Thai fish sauce (nam pla)

salt and pepper

Serves: 4–6

Preparation time: 15 minutes, plus draining and soaking time

hot and sour
noodle and
vegetable salad

A fresh tasting Thai-style salad made with the clear rice noodles available in many larger supermarkets or oriental stores.

- Sprinkle the cucumber with a little salt and set aside to drain for 30 minutes. Soak the noodles, covered, in boiling water for 4–6 minutes, or according to the packet instructions. Wash and dry the cucumber and drain and dry the noodles.
- Combine all the dressing ingredients together, season with salt and pepper to taste and toss half with the noodles. Place in a large bowl.
- Cut the cucumber into long thin julienne strips and add to the noodles together with the julienne strips of carrot and chilli.   Stir in the coriander and the remaining dressing and serve at once garnished with coriander sprigs.

Summertime heralds the arrival of picnics and eating al fresco; this chapter provides a whole range of exciting picnic foods. Wrap up the homemade Olive Foccacia with Infused Herb Oil and include some extra oil to dip the bread into, or really impress your friends with the stunning Picnic Chicken Loaf.

breads
and pastries

Serves: 4
Preparation time: 15–20 minutes, plus resting time
Cooking time: 10 minutes

prawn and rocket
piadina

Piadina is the precursor of the pizza and is a small disc of unleavened dough that is dry-fried on a very hot griddle.

125 g/4 oz plain flour
½ teaspoon salt
5 g/¼ oz butter, softened

Topping:
4 tablespoons extra virgin
    olive oil, plus extra for
    serving
2 large garlic cloves, crushed
pinch crushed chilli flakes
½ teaspoon dried oregano
500 g/1 lb medium-sized fresh
    tiger prawns, de-veined
175 g/6 oz rocket
175 g/6 oz feta cheese,
    crumbled
pepper

- Sift the plain flour and salt into a bowl, make a well in the centre and work in the butter and 65 ml/2½ fl oz tepid water to form a soft dough. Knead on a lightly floured surface for 10 minutes. Wrap in cling film and leave to rest for 30 minutes.
- Divide the dough into 4 pieces and roll each one out to 12.5 cm/5 inch round.
- Cover with a clean tea towel while preparing the topping.
- Heat the oil in a large frying pan and as soon as it stops foaming add the garlic, chilli flakes and dried oregano, stir well and immediately add the prawns. Cook for 3–4 minutes until the prawns are cooked. Stir in the rocket and cook until wilted. Keep warm.
- Heat a griddle or heavy-based frying pan until hot. Cook 1 piadina dough base at a time for about 1 minute, flip over and cook the underneath for a further 30 seconds until dotted brown.
- Transfer the piadina to warmed plates and top with the prawn and rocket mixture, scatter over the feta, serve at once drizzled with extra olive oil.

250 g/8 oz ricotta

1 small garlic clove, crushed

2 spring onions, finely chopped

2 teaspoons lemon juice

25 g/1 oz sun-dried tomatoes in oil, drained and finely chopped

4 tablespoons chopped fresh herbs to include; basil, chervil, chives, dill, mint and parsley

1 small French stick, sliced

4 tablespoons olive oil

1 tablespoon Chilli Oil (see page 119)

salt and pepper

To Serve:

extra virgin olive oil

lemon juice

Serves: 10
Preparation time: 12 minutes, plus infusing time
Cooking time: 3–4 minutes

ricotta *crostini*

- In a bowl beat together all the ingredients except for the bread, olive oil and chilli oil. Season to taste with salt and pepper and set aside for at least 1 hour for the flavours to develop.
- Prepare the crostini. Cut the French bread into 20 slices, about 5 mm (¼ inch) thick. Combine the oils and heat together in large frying pan. Fry the bread slices in batches over a gentle heat until lightly golden on both sides. Drain on kitchen paper and leave to cool.
- Spread a little of the ricotta mixture onto each crostini, drizzle over a little lemon juice and extra virgin olive and serve at once.

pear, chicory and gorgonzola bruschetta

2 heads chicory

50 g/2 oz butter

2 large ripe pears, cored and sliced

4 slices rustic Italian bread, preferably 1 day old

1 garlic clove, peeled but left whole

2 tablespoons walnut oil

175 g/6 oz gorgonzola cheese, diced

salt and pepper

- Trim the outer leaves from the chicory and discard. Cut each one lengthways into 4 slices.
- Melt half the butter in a frying pan and fry the pear slices for 2–3 minutes until lightly browned on both sides. Remove with a slotted spoon and set aside.
- Add the reserved butter to the pan and fry the chicory for 5 minutes on each side until softened and golden.
- Meanwhile, grill the bread under a preheated grill for 1 minute on each side. Rub all over each side with the garlic and then drizzle liberally with the walnut oil.
- Top each bruschetta with the cooked chicory and pear slices, place the diced cheese over the pears and return to the grill for 1–2 minutes until bubbling and golden. Serve at once.

Serves: 4
Preparation time: 25 minutes
Cooking time: 10 minutes

250 g/8 oz puff pastry, defrosted if frozen
1 small Reblochon cheese
1 quantity Egg Glaze (see page 73)
Sweet and Sour Onion Salsa, (see page 92)
  or a sweet chutney, to serve

Serves: 6–8
Preparation time: 10 minutes, plus chilling time
Cooking time: 20 minutes

baked Reblochon

Reblechon is a French semi-soft cows' milk cheese which is disc shaped, about 12.5 cm/5 inches in diameter and roughly 2.5 cm/1 inch high.

- Divide the pastry in half and roll each half out on a lightly floured surface to form a thin square.
- Take the cheese and using a very sharp knife cut away the rind. Sit the Reblochon in the middle of one pastry square, brush around the cheese with a little egg glaze and then top with the second pastry square. Press all around the edges to seal well and then trim the pastry to give a 2.5 cm/1 inch border.
- Transfer the pastry to a baking sheet and leave to chill for 30 minutes. Brush the top and sides with the egg glaze and score the top with a sharp knife to form a criss-cross pattern. Cut 2 small slits in the top to allow steam to escape.
- Bake in a preheated oven, 220°C (425°F), Gas Mark 7, for 20 minutes until the pastry is puffed up and golden. Allow to stand for about 10 minutes, cut into wedges and serve with some salsa or chutney.

1 small head radicchio

125 g/4 oz fontina cheese, rind removed

2–3 tablespoons olive oil

4 slices rustic Italian bread, preferably a day old

1 garlic clove, peeled but left whole

4 tablespoons Anchoïade (see page 124)

salt and pepper

shavings of fresh Parmesan cheese, to serve

Serves: 4
Preparation time: 10 minutes
Cooking time: 5 minutes

grilled radicchio and fontina bruschetta
with anchoïade

- Trim the radicchio discarding any discoloured leaves. Cut lengthways into quarters, wash and leave to dry. Cut the fontina into thin slices and slip in between the leaves of the radicchio.
- Heat half the oil in a large frying pan, add the radicchio and fry gently for 2–3 minutes, carefully turn and cook for a further 2 minutes until the radicchio is golden and the cheese is melted.
- Meanwhile, grill or toast the bread on both sides and rub all over with the garlic clove, drizzle with a little extra oil and spread each one with the Anchoïade. Season with salt and pepper.
- Top each bruschetta with the radicchio, scatter over the Parmesan and then serve at once.

2 red peppers

1 short French stick

1–2 garlic cloves, left whole

8 tablespoons extra virgin
olive oil

1 tablespoon balsamic or
sherry vinegar

4 ripe tomatoes, sliced

150 g/5 oz buffalo mozzarella,
sliced

12 large basil leaves

salt and pepper

Serves: 20

Preparation time: 30 minutes, plus overnight chilling time

Cooking time: 15–20 minutes

pan bagnat slices

Pan bagnat, a Niçoise stuffed bread translates literally as 'wet bread'. A loaf is hollowed out, soaked with oil, stuffed and then put back together. It makes a great picnic dish as well as a snack.

- Place the red peppers on a foil-lined grill pan and grill under a preheated grill for 15–20 minutes, turning frequently until charred on all sides. Transfer to a plastic bag and leave until cool enough to handle.
- Meanwhile, cut the French stick in half horizontally and scoop out and discard most of the middle, leaving a good 1 cm/½ inch thick edge. Leave to one side to dry out slightly.
- Peel and deseed the peppers over a bowl to catch the juices and cut the flesh into quarters. Rub the insides of the French stick with garlic and drizzle generously with the oil and vinegar.
- Arrange the peppers, tomato slices, mozzarella slices and basil in layers in one half of the French stick, seasoning with salt and pepper. Pour over the reserved pepper juices and any remaining olive oil.
- Replace the remaining half of the bread, wrap tightly in cling film and leave to chill overnight. Return to room temperature and cut the bread into 2.5 cm/1 inch thick slices to serve.

Serves: 6
Preparation time: 20 minutes, plus chilling time
Cooking time: 25 minutes

mini pissaladière

4 tablespoons olive oil

1 kg/2 lb onions, thinly sliced

2 garlic cloves, crushed

2 teaspoons chopped fresh
  thyme

1 teaspoon salt

1 teaspoon sugar

3 anchovy fillets, halved
  lengthways

6 pitted black olives

3 tablespoons freshly grated
  Parmesan cheese

Pastry:

125 g/4 oz plain flour

¼ teaspoon salt

50 g/2 oz butter, diced

A classic Provençal tart which can be made with a pizza dough as the base or with a pastry case. The topping however is always the same – caramelized onions, anchovies and olives.

- Make the pastry. Sift the flour and salt into a bowl and rub in the butter until the mixture resemble fine breadcrumbs. Work in 1–2 tablespoons iced water, enough to form a soft dough. Knead lightly and chill for 30 minutes.
- Heat the oil in a heavy-based frying pan and fry the onions, garlic, thyme, salt and sugar for about 25 minutes until golden and caramelized. Set aside to cool.
- Divide the pastry into 6 pieces, roll each piece out on a lightly floured surface and use to line 6 x 7 cm/3 inch tartlet tins. Prick the bases with a fork and chill for a further 20 minutes.
- Line each pastry case with baking parchment and baking beans and bake blind in a preheated oven, 200°C (400°F), Gas Mark 6, for 15 minutes. Remove the beans and parchment. Leave the oven on.
- Divide the onion mixture between the pastry cases, garnish the tops of each one with a cross of anchovies and an olive. Sprinkle over the Parmesan and bake for 10 minutes. Cool on a wire rack and serve warm.

Serves: 4
Preparation time: 5 minutes
Cooking time: 2 minutes

anchovy toasts
with fried green tomatoes

4 green tomatoes
2–3 tablespoons coarse
    cornmeal
2 tablespoon olive oil
4 slices rustic bread

Anchovy Butter:
50 g/2 oz butter, softened
25 g/1 oz anchovies, chopped
2 garlic cloves, crushed
1 teaspoon lemon juice
pepper

Green tomatoes are just unripe red ones, and cooking them is the only way to make use of them. They are often made into a chutney. Here they are coated in cornmeal and fried until just soft.

- First make the anchovy butter: in a blender or food processor purée together the butter, anchovies, garlic and lemon juice and season with a little black pepper.
- Cut the tomatoes into 5 mm/¼ inch thick slices and coat them with the cornmeal. Heat the oil in a non-stick frying pan and fry the tomatoes for a few seconds on each side until golden but not falling apart.
- Meanwhile, toast the bread on each side either over charcoals or under a grill, spread each slice with the anchovy butter. Top with the cooked tomatoes and serve at once.

Serves: 8
Preparation time: 10 minutes
Cooking time: 10–15 minutes

smoked mozzarella and tomato puff tartlets

250 g/8 oz puff pastry,
  defrosted if frozen

2 large ripe tomatoes

125 g/4 oz smoked mozzarella

2 tablespoons Pesto Sauce
  (see page 120)

salt and pepper

Smoked mozzarella is available from good cheese shops or Italian delicatessens. Use another smoked cheese or plain mozzarella as an alternative.

- Divide the pastry into 8 equal pieces. Roll each one out thinly on a lightly floured surface and using a 10 cm/4 inch pastry cutter stamp out 8 circles of pastry. Prick the pastry circles with a fork. Place on baking sheets.
- Cut each tomato into 4 slices and the mozzarella into 8 slices. Spread each circle of pastry with pesto, leaving a thin border around the edges. Top with a slice of tomato and then a slice of mozzarella. Season with salt and pepper.
- Bake the tartlets at the top of a preheated oven, 220°C (425°F), Gas Mark 7, for 10–15 minutes until puffed up and golden. Serve warm.

Makes: 2 oval breads
Preparation time: 5 minutes, plus rising time
Cooking time: 25 – 30 minutes

olive foccacia
with infused herb oil

500 g/1 lb strong plain flour
2 teaspoons fast acting dried yeast
2 teaspoons sea salt, plus extra for scattering
½ teaspoon caster sugar
4 tablespoons Infused Herb Oil (see page 119)
50 g/2 oz pitted black olives, roughly chopped
extra virgin olive oil, to serve

- Sift the flour into the bowl of a food mixer and stir in the yeast, salt and sugar. Then with the dough hook turning gradually add 300 ml/½ pint warm water and half the infused oil to form a soft dough. Knead for 10 minutes. If you want to make the dough by hand, sift the flour into a bowl and stir in the yeast, salt and sugar. Make a well in the centre and gradually work in half of the infused oil and the 300 ml/½ pint warmed water, to form a soft dough. Turn out and knead on a lightly floured surface for 10 minutes.
- Cover the bowl with cling film and leave to rise in a warm place for about 1 hour until doubled in size.
- Knock back the dough, divide in half and roll each half out to a 1 cm/½ inch thick oval. Transfer to two greased baking sheets, cover with oiled cling film and leave to rise for a further 30 minutes.
- Remove the cling film and press indentations all over the surface of each dough oval with your fingers. Scatter over a little extra sea salt, the olives and drizzle over the remaining herb oil.
- Bake in a preheated oven, 220°C (425°F) Gas Mark 7, for 25–30 minutes until risen and golden. Cool slightly and serve warm cut into fingers with a bowl of extra virgin olive oil to dip.

Serves: 12
Preparation time: 20 minutes, plus marinating and overnight chilling time
Cooking time: 20 minutes

picnic chicken *loaf*

4 chicken breast fillets, skinned

4 boneless chicken thigh pieces, skinned

1 tablespoon lemon juice

½ teaspoon ground turmeric

2 tablespoons olive oil

3 tablespoons chopped fresh herbs

50 g/2 oz pistachio nuts, toasted and roughly chopped

1 large round eastern-style sesame loaf

250 g/8 oz chicken liver pâté

salt and pepper

This stuffed bread is weighted down overnight which enables it to be cut into wedges to serve. You will need a round loaf approximately 30 cm/12 inches in diameter.

- Wash and dry the chicken pieces and rub all over with lemon juice, turmeric, half the oil and season with salt and pepper. Leave to marinate for 1 hour.
- Heat the remaining oil in a frying pan and fry the chicken for 5 minutes until golden on both sides. Add 75 ml/3 fl oz water, bring to the boil, cover and simmer gently for 15 minutes. Leave to cool in the pan.
- Remove the chicken and cut it into strips, reserving the pan juices. Place the chicken in a bowl and stir in the herbs, nuts and reserved juices.
- Cut the top from the loaf and scoop out the middle, leaving a 2.5 cm/1 inch thick shell. (You could make breadcrumbs from the filling and freeze for later use if you like.)
- Spoon half the chicken into the hollow bread and carefully spread the pâté over the top. Add the remaining chicken and replace the bread lid. Wrap the loaf tightly in cling film, weigh down with a heavy object and leave to chill overnight. Cut into wedges to serve.

Serves: 8–10
Preparation time: 30 minutes, plus resting time
Cooking time: 3–4 minutes each batch

deep-fried ravioli pockets

Pasta Dough:
250 g/8 oz pasta flour
1 teaspoon salt
2 eggs, plus 1 egg yolk
1 tablespoon extra virgin
   olive oil

Filling:
100 g/3½ oz soft goats'
   cheese, diced
75 g/3 oz chopped cooked
   spinach, squeezed dry
2 tablespoons freshly grated
   Parmesan cheese
a little grated nutmeg
salt and pepper
vegetable oil, for deep-frying

If you have one, use a pasta machine to roll the pasta dough out into long thin strips. Rolling by hand takes longer, but whichever method you choose, it is important that the dough should be very thin, before it is stuffed and fried.

- Start by making the pasta dough. Sift the flour and salt into a bowl, make a well in the centre and gradually work in the eggs, egg yolk, olive oil and enough cold water, about 1–2 tablespoons, to form a soft dough.
- Knead on a lightly floured surface for 5 minutes until smooth, wrap in cling film and rest for 30 minutes.
- Meanwhile, prepare the filling; combine all the ingredients together in a bowl and season to taste with salt and pepper.
- Divide the pasta dough in half and roll one half out as thinly as possible. Place heaped teaspoons of the filling 2.5 cm/1 inch apart over the dough.
- Roll out the remaining dough until slightly larger than the first. Dampen around the mounds of filling with a pastry brush and top with the second layer of dough, pressing down firmly around each mound of filling. Using a pastry wheel, cut each mound into a ravioli square.
- Heat 5 cm/2 inches vegetable oil in a deep saucepan until it reaches 180–190°C (350–375°F), or until a cube of bread browns in 30 seconds. Deep-fry the ravioli in batches for 3–4 minutes until crisp and golden. Drain on kitchen paper and serve hot.

Serves: 16–18
Preparation time: 20 minutes, plus rising time
Cooking time: 2–3 minutes each batch

fried little pizza pies

2 tablespoons olive oil,
1 garlic clove, crushed
175 g/6 oz onions, sliced
25 g/1 oz anchovy fillets in oil,
   drained and chopped
65 g/1½ oz black olives, pitted
   and chopped
1 tablespoons capers, chopped

Pizza Dough:
250 g/8 oz strong plain flour
1 teaspoon sea salt
1 teaspoon fast-acting dried
   yeast
1 tablespoon extra virgin
   olive oil
salt and pepper
vegetable oil, for shallow-frying

For these little pies a mixture similar to the topping of a Pissaladière (see page 105) is used as a stuffing for small rounds of bread dough. These are then formed into crescent-shaped parcels and shallow-fried.

- Make the pizza dough. Sift the flour into the bowl of a food mixer, stir in the salt and yeast and then gradually beat in the oil and 150 ml/¼ pint warm water to form a soft dough. Knead on a lightly floured surface for 10 minutes. If you want to make the dough by hand, sift the flour into a bowl and stir in the flour and yeast. Make a well in the centre and gradually work in the oil and 150 ml/¼ pint warm water to form a soft dough. Turn out and knead on a lightly floured surface for 10 minutes.

- Place the dough in an oiled bowl, cover and leave to rise in a warm place until doubled in size, about 1 hour.

- For the topping, heat the oil in a frying pan and fry the garlic and onions for 10–15 minutes until softened and lightly golden. Stir in the remaining ingredients, season to taste with salt and pepper and set aside to cool.

- Divide the dough in half and roll each piece out on a lightly floured surface to a thin circle about 2.5 mm/⅛ inch thick. Using a 8 cm/3½ inch pastry cutter stamp out 16–18 rounds.

- Spoon a little of the onion mixture into the middle of each round, brush the edges with water, fold over and press together firmly to seal.

- Heat a shallow layer of oil in a frying pan and fry the pizza parcels in batches for 2–3 minutes on each side until golden and puffed up. Sprinkle over a little salt and serve hot.

Serves: 4
Preparation time: 25 minutes
Cooking time: 5 minutes

aubergine and **pepper layer**

1 aubergine
4 tablespoons extra virgin
   olive oil
2 large red peppers, quartered
4 slices day old rustic bread
1 garlic clove, peeled but left
   whole
1 ripe tomato, halved
175 g/6 oz chèvre cheese
pepper

- Cut the aubergine into 5 mm/¼ inch slices, brush with oil and cook under a preheated grill for 2–3 minutes on each side until charred and tender. Let cool.
- Grill the peppers for 4–5 minutes each side. Transfer to a plastic bag; let soften for 15 minutes. Peel and discard the charred skins, cut the flesh into wide strips.
- Toast the bread on both sides and rub all over the surface firstly with the garlic clove and then with the tomato.
- Brush over any remaining oil and layer the aubergine and peppers over the toast. Cut the goats' cheese into 8 slices and arrange 2 slices on top of each toast. Season with pepper.
- Return to the grill for 1–2 minutes until the cheese is bubbling and melted, serve at once.

spinach and ricotta **tartlets**

175 g/6 oz plain flour
a pinch of salt
75 g/3 oz butter, diced
4 tablespoon freshly grated
   Parmesan cheese
3–4 tablespoons cold water

Filling:
125 g/4 oz frozen leaf spinach,
   defrosted and squeezed dry
200 g/7 oz ricotta
2 tablespoons freshly grated
   Parmesan cheese
a little grated nutmeg
2 eggs, beaten
4 tablespoons single cream
salt and pepper

- Sift the flour and salt into a bowl and using your fingertips, rub in the butter until the mixture resembles fine breadcrumbs. Stir in the Parmesan and then gradually work in enough water to form a soft dough. Knead lightly, wrap in cling film and leave to rest for 30 minutes.
- Divide the rested dough into 6 and roll each piece out to line a 8.5 cm/3½ inch tartlet tin. Prick the base with a fork and chill for a further 20 minutes.
- Meanwhile, prepare the filling; place all the ingredients in a bowl and mix until well blended. Season well with salt and pepper.
- Line the pastry cases with baking parchment and baking beans and bake in a preheated oven, 200°C (400°F), Gas Mark 6, for 10 minutes. Remove the foil and beans and bake for a further 10 minutes until the pastry is crisp and golden.
- Divide the filling between the cases, return to the oven and cook for 20 minutes more until risen and firm to the touch. Cool slightly and serve warm.

Serves: 6
Preparation time: 30 minutes, plus resting and chilling time
Cooking time: 40 minutes

1 baguette or ciabatta loaf
3–4 tablespoons extra virgin
   olive oil

For the pesto:
1½ fresh basil leaves
1–2 garlic cloves
2 tablespoons pine nuts, lightly
   toasted
2 tablespoons finely grated
   Parmesan cheese
1 tablespoon finely grated
   Pecorino Sardo cheese
100 ml/3½ fl oz virgin olive oil
salt and pepper

For the topping:
50 g/2 oz pitted black olives
2 tomatoes, peeled
½ small onion
1 garlic clove, peeled
½ tablespoon chopped parsley
½ tablespoon chopped basil
10–12 anchovy fillets
salt and pepper
6 basil leaves, to garnish

Makes: 6 crostini
Preparation time: 15 minutes
Cooking time: 6 minutes

crostini *with*
mediterranean topping

- Start by preparing the pesto. Put the basil, garlic, pine nuts and a pinch of salt in a mortar and grind with a pestle until a paste forms. Alternatively use a blender or food processor or chop with a mezzaluna. Add the cheeses and mix in well.
- Slowly pour in the oil, stirring vigorously with a wooden spoon. Add salt and pepper to taste. The pesto can be kept in a tightly covered jar in the refrigerator for up to a week.
- Next make the topping. Mix together the olives, tomatoes, onion, garlic and herbs.
- Cut the bread at an angle into 6 x 1 cm/½ inch slices and arrange on an oiled baking tray. Bake the slices in a preheated oven, 200°C (400°F), Gas Mark 6, for 5–6 minutes, until the bread is golden brown.
- Spread a layer of pesto on each slice then spoon the topping mixture evenly onto the bread. Arrange 2 or 3 anchovy fillets on each slice. Garnish with basil leaves and serve immediately.

prosciutto and
mozzarella toasts

4 thick slices farmhouse bread
1 tablespoon olive oil
4 slices prosciutto
2 ripe plum tomatoes, sliced
250 g/8 oz mozzarella cheese,
   sliced
1 teaspoon dried oregano
25 g/1 oz pitted black olives,
   halved
salt and pepper

- Lightly toast the bread on both sides and transfer to a baking sheet.
- Heat the olive oil in a frying pan, add the prosciutto and fry over a high heat for 1–2 minutes until crisp and golden.
- Arrange the prosciutto over the toast and top with slices of tomato and mozzarella. Scatter over the oregano and top with the olives. Season with a little salt and pepper and then bake in a preheated oven, 230°C (450°F), Gas Mark 8, for 10 minutes. Serve hot.

Serves: 4
Preparation time: 10 minutes
Cooking time: 10 minutes

Although several of the recipes within this chapter
are accompaniments for, or integral to, other recipes
in the book, the Bagna Cauda can make a splendid
centrepiece for a dinner party starter and the Smoky
Tomato Salsa is a great spread for toasted ciabatta
or a French stick.

sauces, oils and dips

Makes: approximately 300 ml/½ pint
Preparation time: 10 minutes
Cooking time: 5 minutes, plus infusing time

smoky tomato salsa

4 ripe tomatoes
1 small onion, finely chopped
1 red chilli, deseeded and
finely chopped
1 garlic clove, crushed
4 tablespoons chopped fresh
coriander
2 tablespoons extra virgin
olive oil
1 tablespoon lime juice
salt and pepper

The charring of the tomato skins adds a wonderfully intense smoky flavour to this salsa.

- Using tongs hold the tomatoes over a gas flame and char well on all sides. Cool slightly and then peel and discard the skin. Halve the tomatoes, remove the seeds and finely chop the flesh.
- Put the tomato flesh into a bowl and stir in all the remaining ingredients. Season to taste, cover and leave to infuse for several hours. Serve as an accompaniment or with vegetable crudités or tortilla chips.

three flavoured **oils**

Pour a little amount of any of the following oils into a small dish and serve with chunks of bread, as a pre-dinner snack.

chilli oil

4 dried red chillies
2 garlic cloves
300 ml/½ pint extra virgin
   olive oil

○ Place the chillies and garlic in a clean bottle and add the oil. Seal the bottle and store in a cool dark place for 1 week. Use as required. The oil will keep for up to 3 months.

Makes: 300 ml/½ pint
Preparation time: 2 minutes

herb oil

1 sprig rosemary, bruised
1 sprig thyme, bruised
2 bay leaves, bruised
6 black peppercorns, bruised
300 ml/½ pint extra virgin
   olive oil

○ Feed the herbs and peppercorns into a clean bottle, pour in the olive oil and seal the bottle. Leave in a cool dark place (but not the refrigerator) for 1 week for the flavours to develop. Use as required. The oil will keep for up to 1 week.

Makes: 300 ml/½ pint
Preparation time: 2 minutes

infused herb oil

2 sprigs fresh rosemary
2 sprigs fresh thyme
2 fresh red chillies
2 garlic cloves
2 strips lemon rind
¼ teaspoon fennel seeds,
   lightly bruised
6 black peppercorns, bruised
300 ml/½ pint extra virgin
   olive oil

○ Place all the ingredients in a small, heavy-based saucepan and warm over a very low heat for 20 minutes. Do not allow the oil to boil.
○ Leave the oil to cool completely and then transfer to a clean jar or bottle. Seal and store in the fridge. Use as required. The oil will keep for up to 1 week.

Makes: 300 ml/½ pint
Preparation time: 5 minutes
Cooking time: 20 minutes

Makes: approximately 300 ml/½ pint
Preparation time: 5 minutes

2 garlic cloves
25 g/1 oz flat leaf parsley
   (leaves only)
15 g/½ oz each basil leaves,
   dill, mint, chives, chervil
1 tablespoon rinsed capers
1 tablespoon red wine vinegar
1 teaspoon Dijon mustard
300 ml/½ pint extra virgin
   olive oil
salt and pepper

salsa verde

- Put the garlic, herbs and capers in a blender or food processor and pulse briefly until the herbs are finely chopped. Add the vinegar and mustard.
- With the motor running, blend in the oil through the feeder funnel to form a vibrant green sauce. Season to taste with salt and pepper and store in a sealed jar in the refrigerator. Use within 1 week.

pesto

1 garlic clove, chopped
½ teaspoon sea salt
25 g/1 oz basil leaves
25 g/1 oz pine nuts
125 ml/4 fl oz extra virgin
   olive oil
2 tablespoons freshly grated
   Parmesan cheese
pepper

- Put all the ingredients except the cheese in a blender or food processor and pulse briefly until smooth. Transfer to a bowl and stir in the Parmesan. Season to taste with pepper.

Makes: approximately 150 ml/¼ pint
Preparation time: 5 minutes

Makes: approximately 150 ml/¼ pint
Preparation time: 5 minutes

125 g/4 oz pitted black olives
2 garlic cloves, sliced
4 anchovy fillets in oil, drained
  and chopped
2 tablespoons chopped fresh
  parsley
1 tablespoon chopped fresh
  thyme
6 – 8 tablespoons olive oil
pepper

tapenade

- Place all the ingredients except the oil and pepper in a blender or food processor and pulse until you have a fairly smooth paste.
- Transfer to a bowl and stir in the oil. Season with pepper to taste and store in a screw top jar in the refrigerator for up to 1 week.

skordalia

This is a Greek garlic sauce and is served as a dip to accompany cooked meats, fish and vegetables.

- Cook the potatoes in lightly salted, boiling water for 8–10 minutes until cooked.
- Drain well, return to the pan and then heat gently to dry the potatoes out. Leave to cool.
- Using a vegetable mouli or potato ricer finely mash the potatoes until smooth and stir in the garlic, lemon juice and salt.
- Very gradually whisk in the olive oil to form a thick fluffy mayonnaise sauce and season to taste with pepper.

250 g/8 oz potatoes, cubed
3 garlic cloves, crushed
1 tablespoon lemon juice
½ teaspoon sea salt
150 ml/¼ pint extra virgin
  olive oil
pepper

Makes: 250 g/8 oz
Preparation time: 5 minutes
Cooking time: 10 minutes

25 g/1 oz unsalted butter

2 garlic cloves, crushed

25 g/1 oz anchovies in oil, drained and
   roughly chopped

125 ml/4 fl oz olive oil

pepper

a large selection fresh baby vegetables,
   trimmed and blanched as necessary, to serve

Serves: 4
Preparation time: 10 minutes
Cooking time: 10–15 minutes

bagna cauda

This is a hot garlic and anchovy sauce from the Piedmont region of Italy. It is served at the table in its cooking pot surrounded by platters of raw and cooked vegetables.

○ Put the butter and garlic into a small saucepan and heat gently to melt the butter. Cook over a low heat for 2 minutes or until softened but not browned (or the garlic will become bitter).

○ Add the anchovies, stir once and then whisk in the oil. Season with salt and pepper. Continue to cook over a low heat for 10 minutes, stirring from time to time. Transfer the sauce to a warmed bowl and serve immediately with the selection of vegetables.

Makes: approximately 150 ml/¼ pint
Preparation time: 5 minutes, plus soaking time

2 x 50 g/2 oz cans anchovies
    in oil, drained
150 ml/¼ pint milk
25 g/1 oz pine nuts, toasted
2 garlic cloves, crushed
2 tablespoons chopped fresh
    basil
1 tablespoon lemon juice
¼ teaspoon cayenne pepper
2 tablespoons olive oil
pepper

anchoïade

- Place the anchovy fillets in a bowl and pour over the milk, set aside to soak for 10 minutes. Drain and pat dry.
- Roughly chop the anchovies and place in a blender or food processor with all the remaining ingredients except the oil and pulse until smooth.
- Transfer the paste to a bowl and stir in the oil, season to taste with pepper and store the Anchoïade in a screw top jar in the refrigerator for up to 1 week.

2 x 50 g/2 oz cans anchovies
    in oil, drained
150 ml/¼ pint milk
50 g/2 oz canned pimento,
    finely chopped
25 g/1 oz fresh breadcrumbs
2 garlic cloves, crushed
2 tablespoons chopped fresh
    parsley
1 tablespoon red wine vinegar
¼ teaspoon cayenne pepper
2 tablespoons olive oil
pepper

variation
anchovy and
pimento spread

- Use the same method as above, adding the pimentos, breadcrumbs and red wine vinegar to the blender.

Makes: approximately 200 ml/7 fl oz
Preparation time: 8–10 minutes, plus soaking time

Makes: approximately 400 ml/14 fl oz
Preparation time: 2 minutes

mayonnaise

2 egg yolks
1 teaspoon lemon juice
1 teaspoon Dijon mustard
pinch of sugar
½ teaspoon sea salt
300 ml/½ pint olive oil
pepper

- Put the egg yolks, lemon juice, mustard, sugar and salt into a blender or food processor, season with pepper and pulse briefly until pale and creamy.
- With the blade running gradually pour in the oil through the funnel until the mixture is thick, glossy and pale. You may need to add a little boiling water to the mixture if it becomes too thick.
- Transfer to a bowl and taste and adjust the seasoning, if necessary. Cover with cling film and refrigerate until required. This will keep for up to 3 days.

variation
aïoli

2 egg yolks
2–4 garlic cloves, crushed
½ teaspoon sea salt
1 tablespoon white wine
  vinegar
300 ml/½ pint olive oil
pepper

- Combine all the ingredients except the oil in a blender or food processor, season with pepper and continue as above.

Makes: approximately 400 ml/14 fl oz
Preparation time: 3 minutes

index